STARFORCE
HOCKEY

THE GREATEST PLAYERS OF TODAY AND TOMORROW

Eric Duhatschek

A WHITECAP/INSPERO BOOK

WHITECAP BOOKS

VANCOUVER/TORONTO/NEW YORK

FOR MAURICE "ROCKET" RICHARD, A STARFORCE ALL HIS OWN

Published in Canada by Whitecap Books Ltd., 351 Lynn Avenue, North Vancouver, British Columbia, Canada V7J 2C4

Whitecap Books (Toronto) Ltd., 47 Coldwater Road, North York, Ontario, Canada M3B 1Y8
www.whitecap.ca

First Published in 2000

10 9 8 7 6 5 4 3 2 1

Canadian Cataloguing in Publication Data
Duhatschek, Eric, 1956-
 Starforce hockey

Includes index.
ISBN 1-55285-116-8

1. Hockey players--Biography. 2. National Hockey League--
Biography. I. Title.
GV848.5.A1D84 2000   796.962'092'2   C00-910545-X

Created and produced by Inspero Productions Inc., 2464 Haywood Avenue, West Vancouver, British Columbia, Canada V7V 1Y1

Design: CDDC Strategic Communications Inc.

Printed and bound in Canada
by Friesens Corporation

TABLE**OF**CONTENTS

From Joe "The Phantom" Malone to Jaromir Jagr, hockey has always been a game for stars. Great players doing great things on a great stage. Whether it's Georges Vezina or Dominik Hasek stopping pucks, Howie Morenz or Pavel Bure scoring the goals, there is always a group of stars who dominate the game. These stars create the interest, the excitement and the memories of a wonderful sport.

StarForce Hockey takes us under the helmets, behind the masks and inside the stories of the best players in the world. The tales of these players circle the world, from the rinks of Western Canada, Quebec, New England, Minnesota and Michigan to the rinks of Russia, Finland, Sweden and the Czech Republic. The stories unite hockey stars who come from such unlikely places as South Africa, Northern Ireland and Corpus Christi, Texas.

Continuing to grow and thrive, the sport of hockey is always looking to the future. StarForce Hockey takes a long look at the Stars of Today — Yzerman, Joseph, Kariya, and Pronger. Then StarForce Hockey profiles generation next — Tomorrow's Stars — Gomez, Lecavalier, Thornton and company. To top it all off, the Stars on the Horizon, the players few may know now, but all will soon — Jason Spezza, Daniel and Henrik Sedin and other teenaged futures.

Putting it all together shows again that as we follow and love hockey, we follow and thank our stars. This is a great time to be a hockey fan.

PAVEL BURE

JAROMIR JAGR

PAUL KARIYA

PETER FORSBERG

CHRIS PRONGER

NIKLAS LIDSTROM

RAY BOURQUE

PATRICK ROY

MARTIN BRODEUR

DOMINIK HASEK

ROMAN TUREK

MARK MESSIER

OWEN NOLAN

STEVE YZERMAN

JOE SAKIC

TONY AMONTE

TEEMU SELANNE

MIKE MODANO

CURTIS JOSEPH

ED BELFOUR

OLAF KOLZIG

JOHN LECLAIR

JEREMY ROENICK

MARK RECCHI

PAVOL DEMITRA

MATS SUNDIN

SERGEI FEDOROV

AL MACINNIS

ROB BLAKE

BRIAN LEETCH

DOUG WEIGHT

BRENDAN SHANAHAN

VALERI BURE

THEO FLEURY

BRETT HULL

ANSON CARTER

ZIGGY PALFFY

KEITH TKACHUK

JEFF FRIESSEN

ERIC LINDROS

1

STARS OF TODAY

The measure of an NHL star is staying power. Season after season, these players keep popping up on your nightly highlight reels — from Bourque, Yzerman and Modano to Pronger, Brodeur and Turek. Their names may be familiar, but their stories and backgrounds vary greatly. In *Stars of Today*, we tell you about these players' lives and times, identifying the mostly intangible qualities that set the NHL's greats apart from their more human contemporaries.

It is nearing the end of the NHL's 2000 All-Star Game — otherwise known as the Pavel Bure Show — and a television reporter is preparing three questions for his post-game interview with the Russian Rocket.

But what to ask? Mischievously, one colleague offers the solution: "Question 1: Anna Kournikova. Question 2: Russian Mafia. Question 3: Why don't you speak to your father anymore?" Gales of laughter erupt all around at the absurdity of it all. These, of course, are questions the mysterious, mercurial Bure, the NHL's most gifted goal-scoring machine, doesn't generally address.

"I understand people like hockey a lot and want to know things," said Bure. "I am really open and I try to do the best I can to let people know how I play and what I do." But his private life? Off limits.

PAVEL**BURE**

Pavel Bure is the most watchable and the most mysterious star.

PAVEL BURE'S CAREER STATISTICS

Season	Team	G	A	Pts.	PIM
1991-92	Vancouver	34	26	60	30
1992-93	Vancouver	60	50	110	69
1993-94	Vancouver	60	47	107	86
1994-95	Vancouver	20	23	43	47
1995-96	Vancouver	6	7	13	8
1996-97	Vancouver	23	32	55	40
1997-98	Vancouver	51	39	90	48
1998-99	Florida	13	3	16	4
1999-2000	Florida	58	36	94	16
Totals		**325**	**263**	**588**	**348**

A guarded, complex individual, Bure alternately seeks the spotlight and then tries desperately to avoid it. He has been linked to Kournikova in the gossip columns (and in his pronouncements of their engagement and subsequent disengagement); linked to the Russian Mob by a former FBI agent; and years ago, severed all ties with his father, Vladimir, who used to act as his agent and personal trainer.

Bure lives in the South Beach area of Miami. His arrival in the Florida Panthers organization coincided with a dramatic turnabout in the team's fortunes. Others may have more dimensions to their game, but Bure is unquestionably the NHL's most watchable player. In an era dominated by defense, Bure is one of only a few players left with the speed and instincts to

His move to Florida has made Bure a happy hockey player again.

get away on a breakaway on a more or less regular basis. Astonishingly, two major knee reconstructions did little to slow down the Russian Rocket, thanks largely to his unimpeachable work ethic.

Bill Lindsay, a former Panthers teammate of Pavel's, raves about his hockey instincts. "When you've got his kind of speed and your instincts are on, then the puck finds you all the time — and that's not an accident," said Lindsay. "He just knows where to go on the ice. And once he gets even with a guy, he's got him beat. Some players have to slow down to make a play. Pavel does everything in top-flight motion. He is one of the elite players in the game."

The Calder Trophy winner in 1992 and four times a 50-goal scorer, Bure broke in with the Vancouver Canucks in 1991 and led them to the 1994 Stanley Cup finals, where they lost a seven-game heart-breaker to the New York Rangers. Bure eventually became unhappy with Canucks' management — promises he received were broken, he says — and forced a trade that ended a celebrated 1998 holdout.

His presence in Florida helped turn a franchise known for its mind-numbing defensive approach into one of the NHL's more exciting teams. His 58 goals in 1999-2000 were 14 better than the next total. Bure himself will say: "I love excitement." He will also tell you: "I love to try different things." Certainly, it is

INSIDER**FACT**

Pavel and Valeri Bure became the highest-scoring brother duo in NHL history in 1999-2000 season. The top five:

Goals	Family	Season	Brothers (goals)
93	Bure	1999-2000	Pavel (58), Valeri (35)
88	Hull	1968-69	Bobby (58), Dennis (30)
84	Hull	1970-71	Bobby (44), Dennis (40)
83	Stastny	1982-83	Peter (47), Marian (36)
83	Turgeon	1992-93	Pierre (58), Sylvain (25)

"When you've got his kind of speed and your instincts are on, then the puck finds you all the time — and that's not an accident," said former teammate Bill Lindsay.

Even after two knee surgeries, Bure still has the speed and instinct for the breakaway.

difficult, and ultimately foolish, to typecast him. According to Bure, 90 percent of what is written about him is false. Yet he goes to extremes not to set the record straight, preferring to create an aura of mystery around himself.

This may be why Florida is such a good fit for him. Vancouver was a hockey town, and he represented the city's most visible face. Miami is a football town (with a generous helping of South Beach glamour), a place where Bure can lose himself in its many nooks, crannies and beaches. "Everything I've done in life has led me right to here," he said, "so why should I regret anything?"

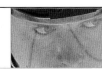

There is a playful quality to Jaromir Jagr that occasionally bubbles to the surface. In his early years, that happened all the time.

Jagr was a laugh-a-minute prankster, just carried along for the ride by Mario Lemieux and all the other great players who helped the Pittsburgh Penguins win back-to-back Stanley Cup championships in the early 1990s. Example: In 1991, in their championship run, reporters surrounded Lemieux's locker, always a grave, serious space, for the obligatory question-and-answer session.

Jagr, amused by the size of the crowd, elbowed his way through and eventually stuck a banana under Lemieux's face, pretending it was a microphone. As Lemieux burst out laughing, all the tension draining out of him, Jagr started peeling his imaginary microphone, as he returned to his own locker with his mission accomplished. Gradually, Jagr's teammates from the championship years disappeared — to retirement or to other NHL outposts — leaving him older, wiser and now, with considerably less hair flowing out of the back of his helmet. The decision to snip his world-famous locks received about as much notice as his scoring exploits, signaling a new

68

JAROMIR**JAGR**

Still having fun, but he's no longer the laugh-a-minute prankster.

JAROMIR JAGR'S CAREER STATISTICS

Season	Team	G	A	Pts.	PIM
1990-91	Pittsburgh	27	30	57	42
1991-92	Pittsburgh	32	37	69	34
1992-93	Pittsburgh	34	60	94	61
1993-94	Pittsburgh	32	67	99	61
1994-95	Pittsburgh	32	38	70	37
1995-96	Pittsburgh	62	87	149	96
1996-97	Pittsburgh	47	48	95	40
1997-98	Pittsburgh	35	67	102	64
1998-99	Pittsburgh	44	83	127	66
1999-2000	Pittsburgh	42	54	96	50
Totals		**387**	**571**	**958**	**551**

seriousness in Jagr's approach to the game. "I haven't changed just because my hair style did — maybe just a little."

Nowadays, Jagr holds almost a paternalistic regard for his teammates, many of whom also hail from the Czech Republic. As the unquestioned leader of the Prague Penguins, Jagr represents a breath of fresh air, someone skating against the grain of the league's suffocating

checking systems. He has Lemieux-like qualities — from his on-ice vision and unparalleled reach to his ability to thread the needle and complete a 50-foot pass. It is this package that makes a special player, according to Mike Eaves, a former Penguins assistant coach. "It starts with his reach," said Eaves. "He's scored highlight film-goals just because he can use his reach to flick a shot by a goaltender." Then there's his size. "His favorite one-on-one

You can run into Jaromir Jagr but it's not so easy to stop him.

Jaromir Jagr is the first player to win the Art Ross Trophy in three consecutive seasons since Wayne Gretzky did it between 1981 and 1987. The Ross leaders:

Player	(titles)	Seasons
Wayne Gretzky	(10)	1980-87, 90, 91, 94
Mario Lemieux	(6)	1988, 89, 92, 93, 96, 97
Phil Esposito	(5)	1969, 71, 72-74
Stan Mikita	(4)	1964, 65, 67, 68
Jaromir Jagr	(4)	1995, 98, 99, 2000

move isn't to try to beat you with his skill, it's to let you run into his big fanny and he spins off you and takes it to the net," said Eaves. "Plus, he has good eye-hand coordination. For those moments when he does need to move the puck, he can."

Jagr, according to Eaves, added a new element to his game in the summer of 1999. "In my first year, I never ever saw Jags take a slapshot — and when he did, he looked awkward. He worked on it all summer and now, he can

Jagr represents a breath of fresh air, skating against the grain of suffocating checking systems. He has Lemieux-like qualities — from his vision and reach to his ability to complete a 50-foot pass.

A serious side has taken a prominent place in Jagr's makeup.

really rip it. So now he's got a new weapon in his repertoire. Plus, he's continued to fine-tune his one-timer. He never felt he had a very good one. Last year, he was all excited because he was watching John LeClair shoot the puck and he says, 'I've got to put my hands out away from my body' like he does."

Lemieux is now his employer, but Jagr discounts the notion that their relationship has changed. "I only look at him as my friend.

I played with him for seven years." What happens when the two friends butt heads across the bargaining table on a new contract? "He already told me, 'Take a pay cut.' That's what Mario said." Underneath that glib exterior, however, beats an ultra-serious heart. "For me," Jagr once said, "it is the worst kind of sacrilege if you are given some special talent and you don't take advantage of this gift." Eaves nods his head in agreement. "His whole life is geared towards being the best."

In his days as the Mighty Ducks coach, Ron Wilson was once asked: How do you define a superstar in today's NHL? By his exceptional skating skills? Gretzky-ish point totals? A seven-figure contract? "In my eyes," replied Wilson, "a superstar is a guy who makes the players around him better — and that's what Paul does."

Paul is Paul Kariya and it is fair to describe him as a superstar, using anybody's definition. Teemu Selanne, Kariya's longtime linemate with the Mighty Ducks of Anaheim, calls Kariya the best player he's ever played with. The essence of Kariya's game is speed and instinct.

Tom Renney, the former Vancouver Canucks' coach, saw Kariya play as a 12-year-old in Burnaby, B.C. and says even then, "he was a creative, imaginative and intuitive player." For all that, Kariya believes that everything is a learned experience, and Kariya's first six NHL seasons have been one ongoing classroom experience. In his rookie year, after scoring just 18 goals, the coaching staff advised him to

9

PAULKARIYA

Instinct and speed combine to create one very Mighty Duck.

PAUL KARIYA'S CAREER STATISTICS

Season	Team	G	A	Pts.	PIM
1994-95	Anaheim	18	21	39	4
1995-96	Anaheim	50	58	108	20
1996-97	Anaheim	44	55	99	6
1997-98	Anaheim	17	14	31	23
1998-99	Anaheim	39	62	101	40
1999-2000	Anaheim	42	44	86	24
Totals		210	254	464	117

shoot more. The next season, he led the league in shots and became one of only 16 players to score 50 goals before his 21st birthday. In his fourth year, Kariya took a crosscheck across the chin from the Chicago Blackhawks' Gary Suter, resulting in a concussion that kept him out of the 1998 Olympics and put his career in jeopardy. The response: A strengthening program that concentrated on building his neck muscles, an idea he borrowed from boxing champion Evander Holyfield.

Knowing that he was part of the younger generation the NHL counted on to help sell the game following Wayne Gretzky's retirement, Kariya overcame his natural shyness and actively worked to be more open and accessible. Kariya took up juggling to help his hand-to-eye coordination. He endlessly pored over Gretzky videos to learn how to change pace on the ice. On the road, he will occasionally ask permission to use the home team's exercise room so he can get in his weight work.

There's a purpose in everything Kariya does — whether he's juggling or working out.

INSIDERFACT

Paul Kariya took 429 shots on goal in 1998-99, the second highest in history. The all-time leaders:

Player	Team	Season	Shots	Goals
Phil Esposito	Boston	1970-71	550	76
Paul Kariya	Anaheim	1998-99	429	39
Phil Esposito	Boston	1971-72	426	66
Bobby Hull	Chicago	1968-69	414	58

He has won the Hobey Baker Award as top U.S. collegiate player, two Lady Byng Trophies and three times was named to the NHL's first-team All-Star. Over the years, he and Selanne have developed an uncanny chemistry. No matter how many coaches try to separate them to get better scoring balance, eventually they put the two back together. They communicate, as if by telepathy. "I can't explain it," said Kariya. "You don't even have to look. You just know. It's knowing the player you're playing

Over the years, he and Selanne have developed an uncanny chemistry. No matter how many coaches try to separate them to get better scoring balance, eventually they put the two back together.

Perhaps Kariya's greatest skill is making the players around him better.

with and knowing where he will be and when he will want the puck."

For Kariya, the most difficult time in his career came in the months it took for the symptoms of post-concussion syndrome to leave. Acupuncture made a difference in the end — and it was Eric Lindros, another player with a concussion history, who put him on to it. Kariya approached the concussion the way he has so many other issues — by studying all the ramifications of it. In the end, after endless discussions with doctors, he pointed out that every case is different because every person is different. Kariya took steps to protect himself. He wears a mouthguard and an extra layer of padding inside his helmet. On the down days, he considered what life would be like without hockey and was glad that it didn't come to that. "I won't lie to you, there were times," acknowledged Kariya, "where I didn't think things were getting better and I was thinking about other things that I could do."

For Peter Forsberg, school days played out a little differently than for his teenage hockey-playing peers. Forsberg's hometown of Ornskoldvik, Sweden is located near the Arctic Circle and thus when winter descends, so does the darkness — for up to 23 hours a day.

There's not much to do except play hockey, which may explain why a town of 60,000 has produced a who's who of Swedish stars for more than a quarter of a century — from Anders Hedberg and Thomas Gradin to Daniel and Henrik Sedin. Or perhaps you can blame it on the presence of the local gymnasium, a special hockey academy that integrates on-ice practices into the regular, structured school day. No wonder these guys get so skilled.

Growing up, Forsberg and the Vancouver Canucks' Markus Naslund were the two best players of their age group and thus constantly competed against each other. "It was a great way to grow up," said Forsberg. "We were always pushed on the ice because we had great competition. I wouldn't accept losing to Markus's team and he wouldn't accept losing to mine." As teenagers, Naslund was rated ahead of Forsberg and made his national team

PETER**FORSBERG**

21

Forsberg's body grew to match his ultra-competitive nature.

PETER FORSBERG'S CAREER STATISTICS

Season	Team	G	A	Pts.	PIM
1994-95	Quebec	15	35	50	16
1995-96	Colorado	30	86	116	47
1996-97	Colorado	28	58	86	73
1997-98	Colorado	25	66	91	94
1998-99	Colorado	30	67	97	108
1999-2000	Colorado	14	37	51	52
Totals		142	349	491	390

debut earlier. "In one season," said former Montreal Canadiens star Mats Naslund, "Peter went from being a regular player to the best in Sweden."

The son of Kent Forsberg — one of Sweden's top hockey coaches and bench boss for Sweden's 1998 Olympic hockey team — Peter Forsberg was drafted in the first round by the Philadelphia Flyers in 1991. Exactly one year later, he was one of eight players traded to the Quebec Nordiques for the rights to Eric Lindros. Forsberg blossomed as a 20-year-old, the year after he was traded, by adding strength and size to an ultra-competitive nature.

Forsberg joined the Nordiques for the start of the 1994-95 season and won the Calder Trophy, edging Anaheim's Paul Kariya. A year later, he was celebrating his first Stanley Cup with the newly relocated Colorado Avalanche. As a player, Forsberg is typical of the second

At least one GM thinks Forsberg is the league's best all-around player.

INSIDER**FACT**

Peter Forsberg was the first hockey player to appear on a Swedish postage stamp, following his Olympic Gold Medal goal in 1994. He was the first player to bring the Stanley Cup overseas. His father Kent is a former National and Olympic coach and his grandfather, Henneng Sandsquist, is a legend in Sweden for his feats of strength.

generation of Swedes, who don't mind playing in close quarters anymore. Once upon a time, the epithet 'Chicken Swede' was hurled at the early pioneering players. If anyone put an end to that tired old stereotype, it was Forsberg, who bears the surgical scars of his gritty, feisty style — on his shoulders and his thighs. "He doesn't fight, but he does everything but," said Adam Deadmarsh, his long-time linemate in Colorado. "He'll hit you, he'll slash you, he'll take a hit to make a play. He loves getting

Forsberg joined the Nordiques for the start of the 1994-95 season and won the Calder Trophy. A year later, he was celebrating his first Stanley Cup with the newly relocated Colorado Avalanche.

One of hockey's hardest jobs: trying to take the puck away from Peter Forsberg.

in the thick of things. He's a competitor. He battles just as hard as any tough guy."

The ability to cycle low in the offensive zone, as if the puck were attached to his stick on a string, is one of the more underrated elements of Forsberg's game. He is so strong on the puck and turns so well in a confined space that defensemen rarely succeed by stick-checking him. They need to use the body against Forsberg, but because he is so slippery and protects the puck so well, that is easier said than done.

Forsberg is well schooled in every hockey discipline. According to former Calgary Flames general manager Al Coates, Forsberg is the NHL's best all-around player, with no discernible weakness in his game. Deadmarsh concurs, noting: "Peter is just as good defensively as he is offensively. He sees the ice better than most guys. He is very unselfish. Sometimes, he should be shooting when he's passing, but he does it because he always wants to help his teammates."

The Chris Pronger story in three acts: Act 1: He is drafted by the Hartford Whalers in 1993 and immediately is compared to Hall of Famer Larry Robinson. Pronger struggles coming to grips with fame, fortune and a game that whizzes by much faster than junior hockey ever did.

Act 2: He is traded to the St. Louis Blues for the popular Brendan Shanahan and the hard times continue under GM/Coach Mike Keenan. It is Keenan who works over Pronger even harder than the unforgiving and unaccepting St. Louis fans. Act 3: Joel Quenneville replaces Keenan as coach and makes Pronger his captain.

By the age of 25, when some members of his draft class were still trying to establish themselves as NHL regulars, Pronger had already played 500 NHL games and had matured into the NHL's most dominant defenseman. "Some nights," said San Jose Sharks coach Darryl Sutter, "Pronger puts the fear of God into people."

It wasn't always that way. Pronger struggled to establish himself in Hartford, amid lofty expectations. His defense partner that first year, Brad McCrimmon, had played primarily with three other defensemen in his distinguished

44

CHRISPRONGER

Chris Pronger puts the fear in the other guys.

CHRIS PRONGER'S CAREER STATISTICS

Season	Team	G	A	Pts.	PIM
1993-94	Hartford	5	25	30	113
1994-95	Hartford	5	9	14	54
1995-96	St. Louis	7	18	25	110
1996-97	St. Louis	11	24	35	143
1997-98	St. Louis	9	27	36	180
1998-99	St. Louis	13	33	46	113
1999-2000	St. Louis	14	48	62	92
Totals		64	184	248	805

career — Raymond Bourque, Mark Howe and Gary Suter — and thus knew what a treasure Pronger could become, if left to develop properly. McCrimmon kept telling whoever would listen: "He isn't the next Larry Robinson or the next Ray Bourque, he is the first Chris Pronger."

At 6-foot-5, Pronger eventually lived up to his early promise and now represents the new prototype for NHL rearguards. Tough, but skilled, intense but focused, he makes teams pay at both ends of the ice. Pronger was asked: What event triggered his development? "My first year in St. Louis, everything came to a head," answered Pronger. "I was getting booed every night, I was miserable. I was one big mess. Then one day, I just said, 'Screw it, I don't know what I'm worried about, just go out and play the game.' I was thinking negatively out on the ice and if you think negatively, negative things are going to happen. It was

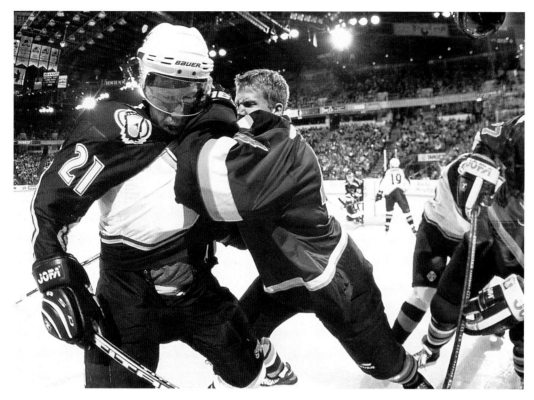

Pronger, applying a hit, took a turn in the right direction when he began trusting his instincts.

INSIDER**FACT**

The St. Louis Blues get their value from Chris Pronger. He's the only NHL player (besides goalies) who has averaged more than 30 minutes of ice time in the two seasons the NHL has kept that statistic. And in 1999-2000 he won his second plus/minus title.

just a matter of trusting my instincts and going with the flow, making what you think is the best decision. And if it's wrong, it's wrong. That's when things started to move in the right direction for me."

There was a time when opponents knew they could goad Pronger into penalty problems by taking advantage of his hair-trigger temper. Now? He's not so easily put off his game. "He was only 22 years old when he first got to St. Louis," said former teammate Grant Fuhr.

"The first Chris Pronger" has matured into the prototype for NHL defensemen. Tough but skilled, he makes teams pay at both ends. His motivation? Getting booed every night.

He may have been No. 2 in the draft but he's No. 1 among NHL defensemen.

"Guys are going to be like that at that age. They need time to mature."

Two years later, Pronger had matured well enough to earn spots on Canada's Olympic team and the NHL all-star team, and he won the league's plus/minus crown. In the 1998 playoffs, Pronger had a scare that made headlines in the Detroit Red Wings series when he stopped a shot on his chest and fell to the ice unconscious. His heart slowed down so badly that paramedics paged his parents to ride to the hospital in the ambulance with him. "It's like I had a little nap," he said. "It wasn't as if I saw a light at the end of the tunnel. There were no angels coming to take me home."

It's too bad Pronger couldn't flash back to that day in 1993 when the prospect chosen just ahead of him in the entry draft (No. 1 to his No. 2) made the following forgettable (and regrettable) pronouncement: "No one," sniffed Alexandre Daigle, "remembers who went second." Oh yes, they do, Alex. Yes, they do.

He was 29 and in the prime of his National Hockey League career when Nicklas Lidstrom wrestled with these questions: Did hockey have priority? Or family?

For almost a year, Lidstrom considered abandoning the NHL to return to Sweden so that his two sons would not be strangers in their homeland. "We were thinking about the kids and if they should go to Swedish schools," said Lidstrom, "but then we talked to some people who lived in the U.S. and then moved back to Sweden and their kids didn't have any problems. So we decided to stay."

The Detroit Red Wings were thankful he did. Red Wings captain Steve Yzerman described Lidstrom as one of the NHL's most underrated players. "He doesn't say a lot, he doesn't get a lot of attention, but he's as good a — no, he's the best — player I've ever played with," said Yzerman. "He's as good a defenseman as there is in the league. He's really our most valuable player and has been for a number of years. He plays 30 minutes a

NICKLAS**LIDSTROM**

Among Lidstrom's biggest fans is Red Wings captain Steve Yzerman.

NICKLAS **LIDSTROM'S** CAREER **STATISTICS**

Season	Team	G	A	Pts.	PIM
1991-92	Detroit	11	49	60	22
1992-93	Detroit	7	34	41	28
1993-94	Detroit	10	46	56	26
1994-95	Detroit	10	16	26	6
1995-96	Detroit	17	50	67	20
1996-97	Detroit	15	42	57	30
1997-98	Detroit	17	42	59	18
1998-99	Detroit	14	43	57	14
1999-2000	Detroit	20	53	73	18
Totals		**121**	**375**	**496**	**182**

game; he plays in all situations. He's good in both ends of the rink. He's the backbone of our team."

For his part, Lidstrom has been one of the NHL's dominant defensemen since he joined the league in 1991-92, perennially finishing among the leaders in scoring by a defenseman. He is also a premier penalty killer and annually a team leader in minutes played. The runner-up for the Calder Trophy in his rookie season, he has been the runner-up in the Norris Trophy balloting, an award no European has won — not even the legendary Swedish defenseman, Hall of Famer Borje Salming. Salming was Lidstrom's idol growing up. "They didn't show many games over in Sweden in

those days, but I read about him in the papers and I even had a chance to play with him in Canada Cup '91," said Lidstrom. "If the Norris would happen, it would be great to be the first, but I don't worry too much about that. I'd rather win the Stanley Cup again than win the Norris."

He may get that chance now that he has elected to stay in North America. "The NHL is the best league in the world," said Lidstrom. "This is where I want to play as well."

It was the fall of 1979 and the Boston Bruins were coming off another good-but-not-good-enough season, when Raymond Bourque turned up for his first NHL training camp.

Peter McNab, who would score 40 goals for the Bruins that season, can recall precisely his reaction when Bourque first stepped on the ice. "Ray was a quiet, quiet kid, who couldn't speak any English," said McNab, "and this was a Bruins team that hadn't had a high first-round pick in a long time. So they dropped the puck for that first scrimmage and the kid was just magic. He was just absolutely the best player right away. There were no growing pains whatsoever."

The rest of the NHL quickly learned what McNab saw — that Bourque arrived in the league as a finished product. He made the all-star team and then did it again 17 more times. He won the 1980 Calder Trophy, in what was arguably the best rookie crop in NHL history and then he added five Norris Trophies as best defenseman.

He also changed the atmosphere and attitude of that Bruins team. "Back then, we used to have a lot of Mondays off," McNab

77

RAYMOND**BOURQUE**

When Bourque arrived, the atmosphere changed in Boston.

RAYMOND BOURQUE'S CAREER STATISTICS

Season	Team	G	A	Pts.	PIM
1979-80	Boston	17	48	65	73
1980-81	Boston	27	29	56	96
1981-82	Boston	17	49	66	51
1982-83	Boston	22	51	73	20
1983-84	Boston	31	65	96	57
1984-85	Boston	20	66	86	53
1985-86	Boston	19	58	77	68
1986-87	Boston	23	72	95	36
1987-88	Boston	17	64	81	72
1988-89	Boston	18	43	61	52
1989-90	Boston	19	65	84	50
1990-91	Boston	21	73	94	75
1991-92	Boston	21	60	81	56
1992-93	Boston	19	63	82	40
1993-94	Boston	20	71	91	58
1994-95	Boston	12	31	43	20
1995-96	Boston	20	62	82	58
1996-97	Boston	19	31	50	18
1997-98	Boston	13	35	48	80
1998-99	Boston	10	47	57	34
1999-2000	Boston	10	28	38	20
1999-2000	Colorado	8	6	14	6
Totals		**403**	**1,117**	**1,520**	**1,093**

recalled. "You'd come down and shower and that was it. Ray started going on the ice and the guys would say, 'What are you doing? This is a day off.' Sure enough, he'd go out there and then another guy did and then another guy. Before you knew it, we'd have these two-hour, marathon scrimmages, East playing against West, and Ray would always play forward. It wasn't as if anybody was there to regulate it. We could have gone off at anytime. But you'd go to go off and Ray would bang his stick, which meant he wasn't through playing — and away we'd go and play some

The highlights in Boston dimmed and Bourque moved on.

INSIDER**FACT**

Ray Bourque ranks third among players in games for a single team. The top 10:

Player	Team	Games
Gordie Howe	Detroit	1,687
Alex Delvecchio	Detroit	1,549
Ray Bourque	Boston	1,518
Stan Mikita	Chicago	1,394
Henri Richard	Montreal	1,256
*Steve Yzerman	Detroit	1,256
Larry Robinson	Montreal	1,202
Gil Perreault	Buffalo	1,191
George Armstrong	Toronto	1,187
Tim Horton	Toronto	1,185
Bob Gainey	Montreal	1,160

* Still active with Red Wings.

more. His enthusiasm was absolutely contagious. Until you play with him, you don't understand how much he likes to play hockey. I've never played with or watched a player who likes to play hockey as much as Ray Bourque does."

For 21 years and through 1,518 games, Bourque played all of his hockey for the Bruins. He made two trips to the Stanley Cup finals — in 1988 and in 1990 — and despite all the personal awards and achievements, those years represented the twin highlights of his playing career.

For 21 years and through 1,518 games, Raymond Bourque played all of his hockey for the Bruins. When he left, he departed with his dignity and class undiminished.

The uniform has changed, but the presence remains.

As a player, Bourque possesses one of the game's hardest and most accurate shots, which helped him become one of only two NHL defensemen in history to produce 400 goals. He can dominate a game physically, in part because he possesses the perfect defenseman's physique — a powerful torso, wide at the hip, two redwoods for legs.

When he left the Bruins in March 2000, traded to the Colorado Avalanche for a chance to win his first Cup, he departed with his dignity and class undiminished. Brian Sutter, an ex-Bruins coach, nicknamed him the Horse, "because that's what he is, a horse. He's a unique, special individual. Good people make good players. Good people aren't people who kiss your rear end every day and say all the right things. Good people are accountable to each other and don't want to let each other down and they make a difference in many different ways."

In the spring of 2000, Patrick Roy began making the rounds of NHL cities with a book under his arm. It was the life story of goaltender Terry Sawchuk, a man who had won a record 447 NHL games in 21 seasons.

Roy, a quirky, offbeat player in his own right, wanted to learn more about the eccentric, troubled Sawchuk — how he won all those games and why he suffered so much doing it. Roy ended the season on the verge of breaking the record.

Roy broke into the league in 1985-86 and promptly led the Montreal Canadiens to the Stanley Cup. That year he achieved notoriety for talking to his goalposts. He called them his "friends," and all through the playoffs they answered him with a comforting "ping," the sound of the puck caroming off the iron and staying out of the net.

Roy was an icon in Montreal during the 10 seasons he played for the Canadiens, the biggest star of his generation. Until Roy's emergence, budding Quebec prospects would take their cues from stylish forwards such as Maurice Richard and Guy Lafleur. In Roy's era that passion changed. "The best players in

33

PATRICK**ROY**

Roy has become the idol of young hockey hopefuls from Quebec.

PATRICK ROY'S CAREER STATISTICS

Season	Team	W	L	T	SO	GAA
1984-85	Montreal	1	0	0	0	0.00
1985-86	Montreal	23	18	3	1	3.35
1986-87	Montreal	22	16	6	1	2.93
1987-88	Montreal	23	12	9	3	2.90
1988-89	Montreal	33	5	6	4	2.47
1989-90	Montreal	31	16	5	3	2.53
1990-91	Montreal	25	15	6	1	2.71
1991-92	Montreal	36	22	8	5	2.36
1992-93	Montreal	31	25	5	2	3.20
1993-94	Montreal	35	17	11	7	2.50
1994-95	Montreal	17	20	6	1	2.97
1995-96	Montreal	12	9	1	1	2.95
1995-96	Colorado	22	15	1	1	2.68
1996-97	Colorado	38	15	7	7	2.32
1997-98	Colorado	31	9	13	4	2.39
1998-99	Colorado	32	19	8	5	2.29
1999-2000	Colorado	32	21	8	2	2.28
Totals		**444**	**264**	**103**	**48**	**2.63**

Quebec, when they are young, want to be goalies," said Francois Allaire, Roy's former netminding coach. By the time Roy left to join the Colorado Avalanche in December 1995, a dozen NHL goalies or up-and-comers had modeled themselves after him, among them Martin Brodeur, Jocelyn Thibault, J.S. Giguere, Marc Denis and Roberto Luongo. In 1993, Roy had backstopped the Canadiens to his second Stanley Cup by winning 10 consecutive overtime games. In 1996, he won for the third time just months after a heated exchange with Canadiens coach Mario Tremblay led to his trade to the Colorado Avalanche.

"The fun part of being in Colorado," said Roy, "is you know you have a chance to win every year.... Winning the Stanley Cup is always

Working in front of his 'friends' has always helped Roy's game.

INSIDER**FACT**

No goaltender has ever won 500 regular-season games. But Patrick Roy has a chance to do so sometime in the 2001-02 season, if he continues to win at a 30-game per season pace, roughly his career average. The all-time leaders following the 1999-2000 season:

Goalie	Wins
Terry Sawchuk	447
Patrick Roy	444
Jacques Plante	434
Tony Esposito	423
Glenn Hall	407
Grant Fuhr	403

the ultimate goal, the ultimate objective that you set out year after year. Maybe because when I was a kid, I was seeing so many Stanley Cups won in Montreal, you always said 'that would be nice if it could happen to me.' And when it happens to you once or twice or three times, you like to see it happen four and five times."

Roy was a second-round draft choice in 1984 after playing for mediocre junior teams in Granby — one year, his goals-against was

Until Patrick Roy's emergence, budding Quebec prospects would take their cues from stylish forwards such as Maurice Richard and Guy Lafleur. In Roy's era that passion changed.

In Colorado, there's always a good shot at another Cup.

an eye-popping 6.26 — so there were no guarantees of a Hall of Fame career. Roy played for great teams, however, and with great teammates through his NHL life. "I should thank them, all the guys over the years," he said. As a player, Roy is known for his candid pronouncements, his guarantees. "I know I am not the best in this business technically or physically, but I always believed in the style that I was playing and it really helped me a lot. The butterfly style, and

stand-up on certain shots, really helped me in the course of my career, but I think the thing that I always loved the most is winning games. I love to go there and put one win on the side and think about the next one and compete and challenge. I just love this game."

In the future, he wants someone to learn about his life and times the way he studied Sawchuk's. "In your first year, you say, 'I would be very happy if I could survive ten years in this league.'" Roy didn't survive; he thrived.

To understand Martin Brodeur's seamless transition to the National Hockey League, it is instructive to remember that, unlike his teenaged peers, NHL dressing rooms held no mystery for him.

Thanks to his father Denis, a professional sports photographer and a fair-to-middling goaltender in his own right, Martin was always around the Montreal Forum to discuss the art of netminding with a procession of goaltenders. His teachers included names like Vladislav Tretiak and Patrick Roy.

And his father had a role too, for Denis Brodeur played for Canada in the 1956 Olympics and used to boast that his son would eventually follow in his footsteps. Martin did, by representing Canada in the 1998 Olympics. Before that event occurred, however, the younger Brodeur had already established himself as one of the NHL's premier goaltenders.

In his rookie season Brodeur led the New Jersey Devils to the Stanley Cup Conference Finals and won the Calder Trophy. In his second year of 1994-95, he did himself one better. A month after celebrating his 23rd birthday, Brodeur hoisted the Stanley Cup over his head.

30
MARTIN**BRODEUR**

By 23, Brodeur had won the Stanley Cup and the respect of teammates and opponents.

MARTIN BRODEUR'S CAREER STATISTICS

Season	Team	W	L	T	SO	GAA
1991-92	New Jersey	2	1	0	0	3.35
1993-94	New Jersey	27	11	8	3	2.40
1994-95	New Jersey	19	11	6	3	2.45
1995-96	New Jersey	34	30	12	6	2.34
1996-97	New Jersey	37	14	13	10	1.88
1997-98	New Jersey	43	17	8	10	1.89
1998-99	New Jersey	39	21	10	4	2.29
1999-2000	New Jersey	43	20	8	6	2.24
Totals		244	125	65	42	2.20

According to defenseman Tommy Albelin, who played with him on the Devils' Cup-winning team, the key to Brodeur's game is his smarts. "With Marty, it's like he's playing chess out there," said Albelin. "He's always four steps ahead of the guy that's shooting on him. He has a great knowledge of the game. As a defenseman, that's very helpful because you knew he would make all the key saves. Your job was to push the forwards as far away as possible to cut down the angle for him."

Brodeur broke into the NHL as one half of a goaltending tandem (with Chris Terreri), but he evolved into a workhorse, routinely putting in 4,000 minutes per season on behalf of the Devils. A two-time Jennings Trophy winner and a two-time all-star, Brodeur has led the league in victories three times in his career and

The best teachers have created a superstar pupil.

Martin Brodeur has the lowest goals-against average among netminders who have played at least 300 games since 1943-44, the year in which the red line was introduced. The five lowest career goals-per-game averages:

Player	Years	GAA
Martin Brodeur	1992-present	2.20
Ken Dryden	1971-79	2.24
Dominik Hasek	1990-present	2.26
Bill Durnan	1943-50	2.36
Jacques Plante	1952-73	2.38

is the only goaltender in NHL history to score the winning goal in a game. That happened in the 1999-2000 season and made him only the second goalie (after Ron Hextall) to score in both the regular season and playoffs.

His ability to handle the puck is one of Brodeur's strong suits. As a youngster, he would play forward on one team and goaltender on another — until he turned eight and was forced to choose between one or the other. "He has probably a better shot than, for sure,

His ability to handle the puck is one of Brodeur's strong suits. As a youngster, he would play forward on one team and goaltender on another — until he was forced to choose.

Brodeur is known for stopping the puck but he shoots it pretty well, too.

I do," laughed Albelin. "If you watch, someone like (defenseman Scott) Stevens is always passing the puck back to him if he's in trouble at the blueline. If you can have someone who acts as a third defenseman back there, then all you do as a defenseman is hold up the forward and Marty will clear the zone or make a good play with the puck." Another strong suit is his attitude — cool on the ice no matter the situation and friendly and approachable off of it.

He has won 30 games or more for five consecutive seasons, something only four other netminders have accomplished. The others: Jacques Plante, Terry Sawchuk, Ken Dryden and Tony Esposito. "That's a great thing to happen, but you feel a little out of place (in that company)," said Brodeur, modestly. That's his view. Others, especially players that play with him, will disagree. "He just seems to get better as the years go by," said Devils center Bobby Holik. "Nobody's perfect — but he's trying to be." Stevens echoes Holik's sentiment: "As a goalie, there's nothing he isn't good at."

For Dominik Hasek, it was all about unfinished business. His legacy of fame will be complete no matter what happens as his NHL career winds down.

There are the world championships, the Olympic gold medal, the Vezina and Hart Trophies, all important achievements in a playing career that began in the Czech town of Pardubice. In what was a highly unusual move at the time, Hasek was promoted from the junior team at age 16 following the defection of Jiri Crha to North America. Through his heroics, Pardubice maintained its position in the first division. Eventually, Hasek became the dominant goaltender in Europe and after a two-year, minor-league apprenticeship, evolved to the top netminder in the world.

Adjusting to the United States proved difficult in the early years because he couldn't speak the language. "I could speak Russian and German, but I never learned English in school, unfortunately," said Hasek. "It is very tough to

39

D O M I N I K **H A S E K**

Finding friends has been a struggle for the intense Hasek.

DOMINIK HASEK'S CAREER STATISTICS

Season	Team	W	L	T	SO	GAA
1990-91	Chicago	3	0	1	0	2.46
1991-92	Chicago	10	4	1	1	2.60
1992-93	Buffalo	11	10	4	0	3.15
1993-94	Buffalo	30	20	6	7	1.95
1994-95	Buffalo	19	14	7	5	2.11
1995-96	Buffalo	22	30	6	2	2.83
1996-97	Buffalo	37	20	10	5	2.27
1997-98	Buffalo	33	23	13	13	2.09
1998-99	Buffalo	30	18	14	9	1.87
1999-2000	Buffalo	15	11	6	3	2.21
Totals		**210**	**150**	**68**	**45**	**2.26**

find friends, even in the locker room or when you go home and you have nobody who can talk. To me, the biggest problem was not knowing the language." Hasek eventually did get comfortable with the language, just as he adapted to the North American playing style. Hasek blossomed after the Chicago Blackhawks traded him to Buffalo for a goalie named Stephane Beauregard and a fourth-round pick. All that's left now — all that motivates the Dominator now — is the quest for his personal Holy Grail, the Stanley Cup. Hasek, who had planned to retire following the 2000 playoffs, rescinded his decision, in a bid to give himself

With a gymnast's flexibility, there are few saves he can't make.

and the Sabres another crack at the Stanley Cup. "Of course, that's why I'm here," said Hasek. "That's why I want to stay this year and next year. I think we can do it with the Buffalo Sabres."

Hasek has become something of an icon in the Western New York area. He has his own hot sauce ("perfect for preparing chicken wings") and his own bottled water. Indeed, in the 1999 Stanley Cup Finals, the Dallas Stars wouldn't use Hasek's brand of water in the Marine Midland Arena dressing room, forcing a luckless trainer to spend all afternoon removing labels to hide the source.

Hasek represents something of a goaltending pioneer. Double-jointed, he possesses a gymnast's flexibility, a characteristic that allows him to drop lower into the butterfly stance than even his most accomplished peers. "The doctors in the Czech Republic always shook their heads when I did that," said Hasek. Unhappily, it is a style that also contributed to recurring groin injuries, which cost him half of the 1999-2000 season. "When I came over to the U.S., I had a tough time because everybody talked about my style being unorthodox. I couldn't prove to them that maybe it is unorthodox, but it is a good style."

Any style that stops the puck is a good style, even if it occasionally involves leading with his face, something Hasek is not averse to doing. He practices using his head to deflect pucks, so when it happens in a game,

INSIDER**FACT**

The only goaltender to twice win the Hart Trophy as MVP, Hasek is also a five-time Vezina Trophy winner. The players to win the Vezina five or more times:

Player	(Trophies)	Seasons
Jacques Plante	(7)	1956, 57, 58, 59, 60, 62, 69
Bill Durnan	(6)	1944, 45, 46, 47, 49, 50
Ken Dryden	(5)	1973, 76, 77, 78, 79
Dominik Hasek	(5)	1994, 95, 97, 98, 99

"I had a tough time because everybody talked about my style being unorthodox," said Hasek. "I couldn't prove to them that maybe it is unorthodox, but it is a good style."

There's always a chance to win with No. 39 in the net.

it happens for a reason. A healthy Hasek is without peer in the NHL. When he's at his best, he leads the team, as he showed in the Olympics in Japan in 1998. Sabres teammate James Patrick put it this way: "With Dom, we have a chance to win every night. He's the best goaltender I've ever played with."

When **Roman Turek was traded to the St. Louis Blues, he had a difficult time containing his disappointment. The deal happened 16 hours after his Dallas Stars won the 1999 Stanley Cup.**

Turek had a chance to sip from the Cup, but by the time they held the parade in downtown Dallas, Turek's name appeared on a different reserve list.

"I was ready for a trade," said Turek, "but I was surprised when Bob Gainey said St. Louis. At that time, Grant Fuhr was still here. I said, 'it looks like I will be back-up again' — because I was sure Grant doesn't like to sit on the bench. Now, I can say I'm so happy I was traded here."

Time — and the chance to be No. 1 on a really good team — tends to heal wounds. Turek had a chance to escape the shadow of Ed Belfour and, at the age of 29, establish himself as a front-liner. In Turek's rise, many observers detect a similarity to Dominik Hasek's. Like Turek, Hasek didn't make an instant impact in the NHL, but needed a full

ROMAN**TUREK**

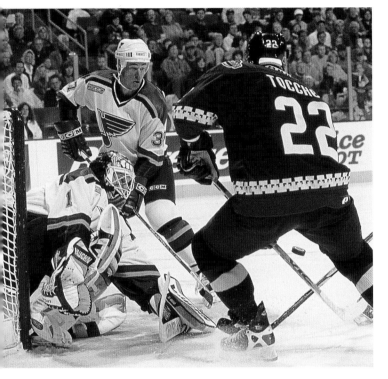

His comfort level in goal was always high.

Season	Team	W	L	T	SO	GAA
1996-97	Dallas	3	1	0	0	2.05
1997-98	Dallas	11	10	1	1	2.22
1998-99	Dallas	16	3	3	1	2.08
1999-2000	St. Louis	42	15	9	7	1.95
Totals		72	29	13	9	2.04

ROMAN TUREK'S CAREER STATISTICS

minor-league season plus a major trade —
from Chicago to Buffalo ironically, also to
escape Belfour's shadow — before he became
a No. 1 goaltender. To Blues teammate Chris
Pronger, the only similarity between the two is
their timetable. "Roman's easier to play in
front of because you know where the rebounds
are going to be," analyzed Pronger. "He's not
flopping all over the place, making the crazy
saves the way Hasek does. Roman's pretty
straight forward along the lines of the way
Grant Fuhr was, just playing his angles and
leaving the rebounds in spots where we could
get it and move it up."

Turek wasn't just the Blues No. 1 goalie, he
was No. 1 in the NHL. It took a dozen games
before Turek adapted, but over the final five
months of the season, the Blues were in sync.
"He's a great handler of the puck," said
Pronger. "He may not get a lot of shots, but
he's figured out a way to stay focused." Turek
became a goalie at age seven when, as a
small, shy boy, he stood at the end of the line
when the equipment was passed out in his
hometown of Pisek, Czech Republic. When
his turn came, all that was left was the
goaltending equipment. "I felt comfortable
there rather quickly," he said.

They call Mark Messier The Moose for good reason. He remains, even at age 39, an imposing, menacing presence.

His shaved head, his granite jaw and a well-defined physique make him one of the most intimidating players ever to play in the NHL. No one currently active in the league has won as many Stanley Cups — six and counting — as Messier. He won the first five with the 1980s Edmonton Oilers, the last of the league's great dynasties, and in 1984, in the first of their championships, he was selected the playoff MVP ahead of his teammate, Wayne Gretzky. The sixth came in 1994 with the New York Rangers, ending that team's 54-year championship drought. If anything put a punctuation mark on his distinguished career, starring on Broadway and then producing a smash hit did it.

Eric Lindros, known in hockey circles as The Next One, grew up idolizing not Gretzky, but Messier. "His speed, his intensity, his drive and his ability to lead is uncanny," said Lindros.

MARK**MESSIER**

11

The look that has inspired hundreds of his teammates.

Leadership is Messier's strong suit, now and always. He would physically intimidate opponents and teammates as well, if they weren't making the commitment necessary to win. "Think of Patton or think of MacArthur," said goaltender Glenn Healy, a former Rangers' teammate. "That's how we feel about Mark."

San Jose Sharks coach Darryl Sutter, who played against Messier for a decade in the 1980s, says he "makes the people around him better." Stephane Matteau, another Rangers alumnus, echoes that sentiment: "For me,

MARK MESSIER'S CAREER STATISTICS

Season	Team	G	A	Pts.	PIM
1979-80	Edmonton	12	21	33	120
1980-81	Edmonton	23	40	63	102
1981-82	Edmonton	50	38	88	119
1982-83	Edmonton	48	58	106	72
1983-84	Edmonton	37	64	101	165
1984-85	Edmonton	23	31	54	57
1985-86	Edmonton	35	49	84	68
1986-87	Edmonton	37	70	107	73
1987-88	Edmonton	37	74	111	103
1988-89	Edmonton	33	61	94	130
1989-90	Edmonton	45	84	129	79
1990-91	Edmonton	12	52	64	34
1991-92	NY Rangers	35	72	107	76
1992-93	NY Rangers	25	66	91	72
1993-94	NY Rangers	26	58	84	76
1994-95	NY Rangers	14	39	53	40
1995-96	NY Rangers	47	52	99	122
1996-97	NY Rangers	36	48	84	88
1997-98	Vancouver	22	38	60	58
1998-99	Vancouver	13	35	48	33
1999-2000	Vancouver	17	37	54	30
Totals		**627**	**1,087**	**1,714**	**1,717**

As the years passed, Messier reinvented his game.

INSIDER**FACT**

Mark Messier is the highest-scoring active player in the NHL and one of only five players in the 600-900 club — 600 goals and 900 assists. The club members:

Player	Goals	Assists	Points
Wayne Gretzky	894	1,963	2,857
Gordie Howe	801	1,049	1,850
Marcel Dionne	731	1,040	1,771
*Mark Messier	627	1,087	1,714
*Steve Yzerman	627	935	1,562

*Active players.

he's the ultimate captain, the ultimate warrior. He's my idol, a great person on and off the ice." In 1999-2000, a simple act of saying he did not want to be traded late in the season fueled the Vancouver Canucks playoff run.

On the ice, perhaps the most under-appreciated part of Messier's game was how he reinvented himself over the last past two decades. He came into the league as a kamikaze and in 1984, during the Oilers' first Stanley Cup run, he helped Edmonton win a pivotal seventh

Leadership is Messier's strong suit, now and always. He would physically intimidate opponents — and teammates, as well, if they weren't making the commitment necessary to win.

The sixth Cup is the punctuation for a marvelous career.

game against archrival Calgary by knocking three Flames players — Mike Eaves, Paul Reinhart and Al MacInnis — out of the game and into the hospital. He was a one-man wrecking crew for much of his first decade in the league.

In the 1990s, his game evolved. Knowing that his body wouldn't hold up unless his style changed, he became less of a goal-scorer and more of a playmaker. He became less of a runaway freight train and more of a graceful,

stylish touring coupe. He is one of only four players in history to exceed 1,700 points, but in the end it is the championships that matter most to him.

"When you win the Stanley Cup six times, it becomes a part of your soul, part of your make-up, part of your identity as a person," Messier said. "Who I am is an extension of my hockey, the way I play and my fever to play the game." That fever is still raging after all these years.

He owns 1,200 acres of land in the hills east of San Jose and they represent Owen Nolan's private place.

Teammates visit, but camera crews that want to record Nolan's life away from the hockey rink are politely turned away. This is where Nolan goes to shoot wild boar, his primary diversion when he isn't sniping goals for the San Jose Sharks.

Off the ice, Nolan's life is simplicity itself. He is, according to Sharks general manager Dean Lombardi, happiest when you give him a gun and "he shoots those pigs he likes to shoot." Presumably, Nolan's aim has been considerably truer in the past 12 months. Belfast-born, Nolan's family emigrated to Canada when he was a young boy, but he didn't start playing organized hockey until the age of nine. Even so, he progressed so rapidly that he was chosen ahead of Jaromir Jagr and Keith Primeau, among others, in the 1990 entry draft.

A perennial 30-goal scorer in the early stages of his career, Nolan — inexplicably, perplexingly — lost his touch around the net for two consecutive seasons. The 1999-2000 season represented a return to form, a re-breakout year that

11

OWEN**NOLAN**

A three-step program has restored Nolan's scoring touch.

OWEN NOLAN'S CAREER STATISTICS

Season	Team	G	A	Pts.	PIM
1990-91	Quebec	3	10	13	109
1991-92	Quebec	42	31	73	183
1992-93	Quebec	36	41	77	185
1993-94	Quebec	2	2	4	8
1994-95	Quebec	30	19	49	46
1995-96	Colorado	4	4	8	9
1995-96	San Jose	29	32	61	137
1996-97	San Jose	31	32	63	155
1997-98	San Jose	14	27	41	144
1998-99	San Jose	19	26	45	129
1999-2000	San Jose	44	40	84	110
Totals		**254**	**264**	**518**	**1,215**

Nolan attributed to three distinct factors. One is the helping hand provided by Vince Damphousse, a true play-making center. Nolan, a tough and hard-nosed winger, opened up the ice for Damphousse. Damphousse, in turn, used that extra space to get the puck to Nolan in shooting position. Two is the presence of Gary Suter, an uncommonly talented power play quarterback, which jump-started the Sharks' play with the man advantage. And three? "I took it easy in the partying department," says Nolan, candidly. It was a heart-to-heart talk with Lombardi in the spring of 1999, followed by a so-so playoff that convinced Nolan something needed changing. So he enlisted in teammate Jeff Friesen's mountain-biking club, hired a personal trainer, and shed the last remnants of baby fat.

Said Friesen: "There's been some tough times for Owen the last couple of years, but he's really found himself now." Nolan seconded his teammate's sentiment: "I just felt when we played Colorado in the playoffs, I thought I could do more, but didn't have the stamina or endurance to do it. So I wanted to make sure that wasn't going to happen again."

It was spring of 1998, some months before the Detroit Red Wings would win their second consecutive Stanley Cup, when Steve Yzerman quietly bought a summer place in Muskoka, the heart of Ontario cottage country.

Yzerman's new home once belonged to Conn Smythe, the former Toronto Maple Leafs owner, which is why he kept the purchase a secret. After all, the Conn Smythe Trophy goes annually to the playoff MVP and Yzerman didn't want to jinx himself or his club. Minutes after the Red Wings completed their Stanley Cup defense — and just as Yzerman received the Smythe trophy from Commissioner Gary Bettman — teammate Brendan Shanahan couldn't contain himself any longer and blurted out the news on national television.

Until the Red Wings captured back-to-back championships, Yzerman was known mainly for personal rather than team achievements. Yzerman joined the Red Wings in the fall of 1983 and, by the end of the 1999-2000 season, was the NHL's No. 6 all-time scorer. During

19

STEVEYZERMAN

His numbers put Yzerman in rare company.

STEVE YZERMAN'S CAREER STATISTICS

Season	Team	G	A	Pts.	PIM
1983-84	Detroit	39	48	87	33
1984-85	Detroit	30	59	89	58
1985-86	Detroit	14	28	42	16
1986-87	Detroit	31	59	90	43
1987-88	Detroit	50	52	102	44
1988-89	Detroit	65	90	155	61
1989-90	Detroit	62	65	127	79
1990-91	Detroit	51	57	108	34
1991-92	Detroit	45	58	103	64
1992-93	Detroit	58	79	137	44
1993-94	Detroit	24	58	82	36
1994-95	Detroit	12	26	38	40
1995-96	Detroit	36	59	95	64
1996-97	Detroit	22	63	85	78
1997-98	Detroit	24	45	69	46
1998-99	Detroit	29	45	74	42
1999-2000	Detroit	35	44	79	34
Totals		**627**	**935**	**1,562**	**816**

that season, Yzerman became the 10th player to record 900 assists and the 11th to score 600 goals. Only four others have ever done both: Wayne Gretzky, Gordie Howe, Marcel Dionne and Mark Messier. Only two players in history, Gretzky and Mario Lemieux, have ever scored more points in a single season than Yzerman did in 1988-89 when he scored 155. To Red Wings coach Scotty Bowman, Yzerman's will-to-win always existed, even if his quiet demeanor sometimes masked that quality to outsiders. It is, according to Bowman, a characteristic Yzerman shared with Lemieux, another two-time Stanley Cup

Hockey's unforgettable moment: Yzerman passes the Cup to his fallen teammate, Konstantinov.

INSIDER**FACT**

Steve Yzerman has scored more goals than any player who has played his entire career in a single organization.
The top five:

Player	Team	Goals
Steve Yzerman	Detroit Red Wings	627
Mario Lemieux	Pittsburgh Penguins	613
Mike Bossy	New York Islanders	573
Maurice Richard	Montreal Canadiens	544
Stan Mikita	Chicago Blackhawks	541

champion, whom Bowman coached in Pittsburgh. "People didn't see that quality in Mario," Bowman said, "but it was there. Just because someone isn't outwardly emotional, it doesn't mean they don't have this burning desire to win."

As Yzerman matured, his offensive numbers have dropped to only about half what they were a decade ago, but he was perfectly willing to sacrifice gaudy statistics in favor of championship rings. "There's always a different perception in hockey of a player who has been on a Stanley Cup winner, and a player who hasn't," said Yzerman. "There's always the perception that this guy has what it takes to win, because he's won, or that this guy doesn't have what it takes to win because he never did. I've never truly believed that and I still don't, but... there's no question, I'm getting more recognition now than ever before."

Yzerman has been captain of the Red Wings since the 1986-87 season, the longest serving captain in NHL history. His attention to the captain's details showed best on the nights the Wings won their Cups. In 1997, he turned and handed the Cup to teammate Slava Fetisov, whose struggle to leave the Soviet Union inspired so many. Then in 1998, he turned and placed the Cup in the lap of injured teammate Vladimir Konstantinov, left wheelchair-bound by an accident following the previous spring's triumph.

As Yzerman matured, his offensive numbers dropped to only about half what they were a decade ago, but he was perfectly willing to sacrifice gaudy statistics for championship rings.

The captains' captain: a new style brought him the Cup.

Ultimately, Yzerman wants to play 20 years in the NHL, which would carry him through until the end of the 2002-03 season. The key to his longevity, says Yzerman, is "playing on a good team with good players. It makes the game so much easier. It makes you a better player, just being on a talented line. It's easier to stay competitive. I really try to work at the conditioning to stay healthy. Guys can play a long time if they take care of themselves. I particularly work on speed, try not to lose that. If you stay relatively healthy, you should be able to play for a while. That," concluded Yzerman, with a twinkle, "plus expansion."

This is the essence of Joe Sakic: In his final year of junior hockey, knowing that the Quebec Nordiques had drafted him, he dropped high school French.

Didn't want it and therefore wouldn't take it, even if Quebec was as close to a unilingual Francophone city as exists this side of Paris.

Sakic is universally known for his soft-spoken nature, but anyone who mistakes his quiet nature for a lack of resolve is badly mistaken. Sakic was toughened up early on in his hockey-playing life. In his first year of junior, he was a passenger on the Swift Current Broncos bus that crashed on an icy Saskatchewan highway, killing four of his teammates. In the aftermath of the tragedy, Sakic played spectacularly and virtually willed the team into the playoffs. Sakic did not seek counseling to cope. "I just dealt with it myself," he said.

JOESAKIC 19

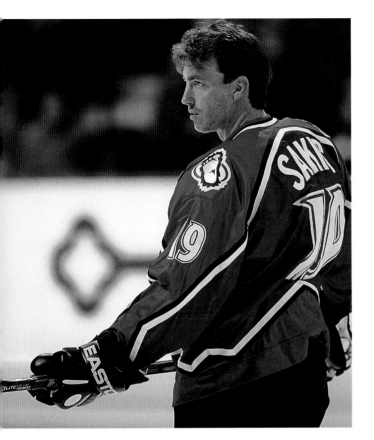

Sakic's life was changed by a bus accident in Saskatchewan.

JOE SAKIC'S CAREER STATISTICS

Season	Team	G	A	Pts.	PIM
1988-89	Quebec	23	39	62	24
1989-90	Quebec	39	63	102	27
1990-91	Quebec	48	61	109	24
1991-92	Quebec	29	65	94	20
1992-93	Quebec	48	57	105	40
1993-94	Quebec	28	64	92	18
1994-95	Quebec	19	43	62	30
1995-96	Colorado	51	69	120	44
1996-97	Colorado	22	52	74	34
1997-98	Colorado	27	36	63	50
1998-99	Colorado	41	55	96	29
1999-2000	Colorado	28	53	81	28
Totals		**403**	**657**	**1,060**	**368**

Sakic's early years with the Quebec Nordiques featured a lengthy, painful struggle for respectability. The losing — four years in a row out of the playoffs — made the good times all the sweeter.

In 1996, Sakic won a Stanley Cup championship in the first year after the team moved to Colorado from Quebec. That magical season, Sakic scored 51 goals and 120 points. In the playoffs, he added another 18 goals, one shy of Jari Kurri's and Reggie Leach's NHL playoff record, and won the Conn Smythe as the playoff MVP.

"Things went pretty good for me that playoff," shrugged Sakic, "for everybody on the team." It is observations like these that

Sakic is a strong, and mostly silent, type of player.

INSIDER**FACT**

Joe Sakic's first three seasons in Quebec produced 110 goals and a plus/minus rating of -102; his last three seasons in Colorado have produced 96 goals and a plus/minus of +53. He was second among NHL forwards in 1999-2000 with a +30.

earned Sakic his nickname among reporters in Denver: Quoteless Joe. Teammate Sandis Ozolinsh says long-time Avalanche players have come to appreciate Sakic's brand of low-key leadership. "You don't have to be necessarily very vocal to be a leader," said Ozolinsh. "Players are aware of what he does on the ice. They see him and they see how hard he works. He's really one of the guys who gets us to where we are in the standings. He's been a real captain for us."

The summer after Colorado's championship season, the New York Rangers tried to spirit him out of Denver by offering him a three-year, $21 million contract that included a $15 million bonus, payable to him the week he signed. The Avalanche, desperate to retain him, needed a week to get their financing in order and eventually matched the offer. Despite his new found wealth, Sakic remained a dedicated athlete with a strong, if deep-seated, will to win.

Of Sakic, a former coach once said: "You never get the impression in talking to him that he's an NHL superstar, because he's not outwardly boastful or proud. He is literally an ordinary Joe off the ice. Sometimes, you can't believe that the Joe Sakic sitting there, kidding around, is the same guy that would go onto the ice. It was like he'd gone into a phone booth or something."

As a player, Super Joe isn't especially physical, but he is an exceptional playmaker and possesses an underrated wrist shot. As a

"Things went pretty good for me that playoff, for everybody on the team," said Sakic after Colorado won the Cup, illustrating his reticence and his low-key leadership.

An exceptional playmaker and owner of an accurate wrist shot.

person, Sakic doesn't talk much about his private life, which he now considers off limits. Once, however, he suggested that the bus crash changed him in ways that were difficult to explain. "For me, it was the first time anything tragic had happened," he said. "I realized then that, at any time, it could be over, so you just take things more carefully. I was more careful in my decisions and in the things I was doing. Instead of jumping up and doing something and not caring, it was like: 'I've got to think of the consequences here.'"

In his early years, the myth surrounding the Chicago Blackhawks' Tony Amonte, he believes, was perpetuated by a curious misunderstanding with New York Rangers coach Mike Keenan.

Seeing his prep school background — he attended prestigious Thayer Academy for four years and played on the same team as Jeremy Roenick — Keenan naturally assumed Amonte was a spoiled rich kid and required constant pushing to achieve his full potential. Actually, Amonte hailed from a working-class neighborhood in Hingham, Mass., son of a construction worker, and made it to Thayer on a scholarship.

Hard work was second nature to Amonte, as he went on to Boston University for two years and arrived in New York, just as the Rangers were going through a significant upheaval. Amonte was third behind Pavel Bure and Niklas Lidstrom for the 1992 Calder Trophy and produced 68 goals in his first two full seasons. In 1993-94, as the Rangers geared up for a Stanley Cup push, they traded Amonte to the

10

TONYAMONTE

This is not the face of a prep school pretty boy.

TONY AMONTE'S CAREER STATISTICS

Season	Team	G	A	Pts.	PIM
1991-92	NY Rangers	35	34	69	55
1992-93	NY Rangers	33	43	76	49
1993-94	NY Rangers	16	22	38	31
1993-94	Chicago	1	3	4	6
1994-95	Chicago	15	20	35	41
1995-96	Chicago	31	32	63	62
1996-97	Chicago	41	36	77	64
1997-98	Chicago	31	42	73	66
1998-99	Chicago	44	31	75	60
1999-2000	Chicago	43	41	84	48
Totals		**290**	**304**	**594**	**482**

Blackhawks for two Keenan favorites, Stephane Matteau and Brian Noonan. Matteau and Noonan won a championship that year, and Amonte's Blackhawks meekly exited the playoffs in six games. Both players acquired by New York settled in as journeymen. Amonte became a star.

"Tony comes to play hard every night," says the Detroit Red Wings' Chris Chelios, a former teammate. "There's no quit in him." Amonte has missed only nine games in his first nine NHL seasons and only two games since the 1994-95 season. He quietly produces a point a game, on good teams and bad, through sickness and health.

"Tony works hard on the ice and that pays off for him," said former Blackhawk teammate Dave Manson. "The fact that he's been able to get it done with a variety of different linemates over the last few years shows you just how consistent he is. He likes to come from behind, so he's always getting the puck with speed. That's his strength. If he buried all his scoring chances, he'd have 60 to 70 goals a year." Three times a 40-goal scorer, Amonte can only concur with Manson's assessment: "I should be scoring 50. Fifty is a goal of mine and as far as being a good player, I think I have to be better because we haven't been in the playoffs the last few years."

He uses the pseudonym Teddy Flash when he is driving the rally car circuit in his native Finland and if Mighty Ducks of Anaheim GM Pierre Gauthier is bothered by Teemu Selanne's crazy hobbies, well, he isn't saying.

Selanne always lived life in the fast lane, growing up in Helsinki, pulling stunts that he should discourage his two children from doing. Press him about his fascination with speed and Selanne will tell you about the game he and friends invented as teenagers. First, they would pile into their cars and drive to the ocean, about an hour away. Next, they'd attach tire chains to their vehicles and tow ropes to their bumpers and themselves. Finally, they'd don their skates or downhill skis and take turns flying across the ice, careening this way and that, a fraction ahead of disaster.

Even now, the mild-mannered Selanne, the NHL's quintessential nice guy, is a maniac about speed. In the summer of 1999, he accidentally ran down the president of the Finnish Ice

8

TEEMUSELANNE

a/k/a Teddy Flash: Speed is part of Selanne's life.

TEEMU SELANNE'S CAREER STATISTICS

Season	Team	G	A	Pts.	PIM
1992-93	Winnipeg	76	56	132	45
1993-94	Winnipeg	25	29	54	22
1994-95	Winnipeg	22	26	48	2
1995-96	Winnipeg	24	48	72	18
1995-96	Anaheim	16	20	36	4
1996-97	Anaheim	51	58	109	34
1997-98	Anaheim	52	34	86	30
1998-99	Anaheim	47	60	107	30
1999-2000	Anaheim	33	52	85	12
Totals		**346**	**383**	**729**	**197**

Hockey Federation on a racetrack. It is not the first time Selanne's motoring caused him grief. In Finland, speeding tickets are assessed as a percentage of a person's income. Selanne's first ticket as a pro cost him the equivalent of $5,000. "Some guys fish in the summer," said Selanne. "I drive cars. You can get hurt fishing too." Maybe if you're trolling for shark.

Selanne burst on the scene in the 1992-93 season with the Winnipeg Jets, when he scored 76 goals as a rookie, shattering the record of 53 established by Mike Bossy 15 years before. It is a record that will likely never be broken. Selanne's second and third seasons were undermined by an Achilles tendon tear that took away some of that speed, which defines his

Pleasingly out of step — in all the commendable ways.

By scoring 76 goals in his rookie season, Teemu Selanne improved Mike Bossy's previous record of 53 by a whopping 43 percent. For another player to break Selanne's record by a similar percentage, he would have to score 32 more goals — or 108 for the season. Wayne Gretzky's single-season record is 92. In other words, it will only happen if the nets become soccer-sized.

game. In the winter of 1996, with the Jets preparing to relocate to Phoenix, Selanne was traded to Anaheim, where he hooked up with Paul Kariya to form the NHL's most dynamic duo. Selanne, outgoing and open, had a positive effect on the quiet Kariya. Anaheim turned out to be a good fit for Selanne, in part because it helps him escape the fevered attention he gets in his native Finland. Selanne has a tattoo on his right ankle of the Finnish flag pierced by a lightning bolt. The tattoo

Selanne is pleasingly out of step. He scores goals when scoring is in decline. He is approachable when others are aloof. He doesn't quibble about money when others squeeze out every dollar.

When it comes to scoring goals, no one is a peer of the Ducks' Selanne.

came during a 48-hour reverie, also known as his stag party, where, among other things, he dressed as an Elvis impersonator and sang hurtin' songs badly in a McDonald's restaurant. The adventure culminated with him at the local soccer stadium dressed in Helsinki's colors and playing in a soccer game for the home club.

Selanne is pleasingly out of step with the crowd. He scores goals at a time when NHL scoring is in decline — and since entering the league, no one has turned on the red light more. In the 1998-99 season, he won the inaugural Rocket Richard Trophy, awarded to the NHL's goal leader. He is approachable when others are aloof. He doesn't quibble about money when others squeeze every last dollar. Kariya says his teammate is the better goal scorer: "I need 10 or 12 chances to get one. Teemu needs one to get one." The other distinct difference between Selanne and lesser mortals is his ability to make plays at top speed, something only a handful of others can do. "Otherwise," said Selanne, "there would be a lot of speedskaters in this sport."

Mike Modano grew up in the Detroit suburbs and as such, had more than a passing interest in the evolution of Red Wings center Steve Yzerman.

Yzerman was considered something of a pretty boy in his early days, but gradually became a strong two-way player and completed his conversion by winning consecutive Stanley Cups. Modano has completed a similar change. In his early days, he was pure offense. He was Mr. Outside who was joined by teammate Joe Nieuwendyk as Mr. Inside. The first player chosen in the 1988 entry draft, Modano used speed and reach to score bushels of goals, but apart from a surprise trip to the 1991 Stanley Cup Finals, he didn't accomplish much in a team way.

When he became the Dallas Stars coach, Ken Hitchcock challenged Modano to develop into the same sort of player as Yzerman became — less pretty, more effective. The scoring totals

9

MIKE**MODANO**

Modano's looks have put him in unusual places for a hockey star.

MIKE MODANO'S CAREER STATISTICS

Season	Team	G	A	Pts.	PIM
1989-90	Minnesota	29	46	75	63
1990-91	Minnesota	28	36	64	61
1991-92	Minnesota	33	44	77	46
1992-93	Minnesota	33	60	93	83
1993-94	Dallas	50	43	93	54
1994-95	Dallas	12	17	29	8
1995-96	Dallas	36	45	81	63
1996-97	Dallas	35	48	83	42
1997-98	Dallas	21	38	59	32
1998-99	Dallas	34	47	81	44
1999-2000	Dallas	38	43	81	48
Totals		349	467	816	544

slid as Modano concentrated more on playing a two-way game. Hitchcock calls this "being the best player on every shift." According to Dave Reid, a teammate of Modano's on the 1999 Stars: "The one thing Hitch brought up in the three years I was there was how Detroit's play progressed. Instead of going for scoring points, they developed a more team game. They started blocking shots, killing penalties, winning the battles in their own

His outspoken comments on player safety have won him respect, too.

zone. That definitely sacrifices offensive time and offensive totals, but in the big picture, that wins championships. Modano's definitely developed that style of play." Modano's evolution was complete when the Stars won the 1999 Stanley Cup and he played the Finals with a broken bone in his wrist. Nothing pretty about that.

"Early in my career, I thought if I wasn't scoring, I wasn't succeeding," said Modano. Hitchcock worked overtime to dissuade him of that notion. In Nieuwendyk's mind, the comparisons between the career paths of Modano and Yzerman "are fair. Mike's going to spend the rest of his career in Dallas, the same as Steve with Detroit. Physically, he's a horse, big, fast, strong, someone who can really shoot the puck. He would be the first to tell you that the year [after the Stanley Cup championship] started a bit ragged for him, but then he really picked it."

The word ragged hardly describes what happened to Modano in the 1999-2000 season. He suffered a concussion in the opening week on an illegal hit from the Mighty Ducks' Ruslan Salei. The suspension handed down to Salei was not enough for Modano. The concussion plus a series of other injuries turned Modano into one of the game's most outspoken individuals when it came to safety. "Do we have to wait for someone to be paralyzed or killed before the league, teams and players come together to act?" he asked. "The result of a

INSIDER FACT

Mike Modano has won a Stanley Cup in Dallas, led the team in scoring six times and is the team career goal-scoring leader with 349. And to show how good an athlete he is, his drive of 379 yards won a long-driving contest, beating the likes of football's John Elway.

Following a series of injuries, Modano has become one of the most outspoken players when it comes to safety, calling for the league, teams and players to come together to act.

Modano found the right role model to reconstruct his game.

professional hockey game should not be that we are lucky to escape paralysis or are lucky to have our eyesight after willful acts of violence."

His presence off the ice has been considerable. He has been photographed with supermodel Tyra Banks for a 1995 *Cosmopolitan* magazine layout. That hockey-reporting bible, *People* magazine, visited Modano and girlfriend Kerri Nelson at his Las Colinas, Texas, townhouse in

1997. It's hard to shake that pretty boy image, even if it no longer accurately sums him up. Some people do not see the broken nose and wrist, the concussions, the sprained knees and ankles. The process was gradual, but even GM Bob Gainey, seen by so many as the ultimate hockey warrior, understands how difficult it was for his star. "He learned to become a good competitor at the hardest times," said Gainey.

Amiable, mild-mannered Curtis Joseph is standing in the Maple Leafs dressing room, offering up the lessons he has learned in his first decade as a National Hockey League goaltender.

How do you go from being a player passed over in his three years of eligibility for the NHL entry draft to big-time star?

"There's the maturity factor," began Joseph. "Work ethic is big. Confidence is big. Once you've been around a few years and get to know the shooters, you start to know all the good players in the league. Maybe," concluded Joseph, thoughtfully, "you just find yourself."

It took Joseph years to do just that. Born in 1967 to Wendy Munro, an unwed mother, he was given up for adoption five days later to Jeanne and Harold Joseph. Quiet and unassuming as a boy, Joseph once described himself as being "scared of his shadow" growing up in Keswick, Ontario, the adoptive son of middle-aged parents consumed by running a group home for mentally challenged adults.

31

CURTISJOSEPH

Only Joseph believed he could play in the NHL.

CURTIS JOSEPH'S CAREER STATISTICS

Season	Team	W	L	T	SO	GAA
1989-90	St. Louis	9	5	1	0	3.38
1990-91	St. Louis	16	10	2	0	3.12
1991-92	St. Louis	27	20	10	2	3.01
1992-93	St. Louis	29	28	9	1	3.02
1993-94	St. Louis	36	23	11	1	3.10
1994-95	St. Louis	20	10	1	1	2.79
1995-96	Edmonton	15	16	2	0	3.44
1996-97	Edmonton	32	29	9	6	2.93
1997-98	Edmonton	29	31	9	8	2.63
1998-99	Toronto	35	24	7	3	2.56
1999-2000	Toronto	36	20	7	4	2.49
Totals		**284**	**216**	**68**	**26**	**2.88**

Hockey provided solace for Curtis and his older brother Grant. Joseph knew early on that he wanted to play goal professionally and he believed he could. But his belief was not shared — in the beginning, anyway — by major junior teams around Ontario. Joseph was largely an unknown quantity as a teenager. With few available options, he eventually found a hockey-playing home in Wilcox, Saskatchewan, and rewarded the faith in him by backstopping the Notre Dame Hounds to a Tier 2 Canadian title. From there, Joseph enrolled at the University of Wisconsin on a scholarship and stayed two years, before signing with the St. Louis Blues as a free agent.

"He was as good a player as has ever emerged out of nowhere at the age of 21," said Ron Caron, the Blues' senior advisor and former GM. General Manager Mike Keenan traded him out of St. Louis to Edmonton in 1995, despite six consecutive winning seasons. Joseph helped the Oilers upset Dallas and Colorado in the 1997 and 1998 playoffs respectively. And then he signed with the Maple Leafs as a free agent.

The education of Curtis Joseph is a never-ending story.

INSIDER FACT

Growing up as an adoptive child has helped lead Curtis Joseph to devote himself to children's charities. For the Sick Children's Hospitals in Toronto, Hamilton and London, Ontario, he donates a suite at the Air Canada Centre. For the Children's Wish Foundation of Canada he sponsors a golf tournament each summer that attracts almost 300 participants.

Says Leafs GM/Coach Pat Quinn: "Not one goalie I've ever been associated with can pick up the defense the way he does." For his part Joseph can tell you, from personal experience, that every development path is different, and that in the NHL, the education process never ends. "The key is to constantly learn," said Joseph. "Learn to be a pro and to develop a thick skin. That's important as a goaltender, getting a thick skin." Joseph laughs: "You're just always gradually, constantly building. You

"The key is constantly to learn," said Curtis Joseph. "Learn to be a pro and to develop a thick skin. That's important as a goaltender, getting a thick skin."

Nothing picks up a defense like Cujo flying solo and making a save.

never want to say, 'I've got this league figured out' because it's constantly changing. Since I came into the league, the game has changed quite a bit as far as speed and its dynamics, so you're ever changing your game to keep pace. You're constantly changing your game to fit this game."

When his thick skin was pierced during the 2000 playoffs, he accidentally knocked a referee off his feet while protesting a goal. Afterwards, he thought first of how his own children would

react. And perhaps because of his reputation, he somehow avoided suspension.

In part because of his background and upbringing, Joseph is a devoted family man who works tirelessly on behalf of children's charities in the Toronto area. Once he signed his contract with the Maple Leafs, he purchased a private box at the Air Canada Centre, in which he hosts kids from three different children's hospitals. His own family didn't get a chance to use the box until the 2000 All-Star Game in Toronto.

The seminal moment of Ed Belfour's career came in the spring of 1999 in the first hours of a steamy morning in Buffalo, N.Y., as his Dallas Stars won their first-ever Stanley Cup.

There, standing beside NHL Commissioner Gary Bettman to receive the Conn Smythe Trophy as the playoff Most Valuable Player, was Joe Nieuwendyk. Moments later, Bettman handed off the Stanley Cup to team captain Derian Hatcher. By the players' benches at one side of the Marine Midland Arena, Brett Hull was outlining his play on the winning goal. Over on the other side, Mike Modano was revealing the extent of his wrist injury, broken earlier in the series.

Belfour, the goaltender who held the creaky and battered Stars line-up together with timely saves throughout the post-season, looked practically forgotten amid the exuberant but exhausted good cheer. For someone who took considerable blame for all of his team's previous playoff pratfalls, it hardly seemed fair

20

ED BELFOUR

Nothing satisfies like proving people wrong.

ED BELFOUR'S CAREER STATISTICS

Season	Team	W	L	T	SO	GAA
1988-89	Chicago	4	12	3	0	3.87
1990-91	Chicago	43	19	7	4	2.47
1991-92	Chicago	21	18	10	5	2.70
1992-93	Chicago	41	18	11	7	2.59
1993-94	Chicago	37	24	6	7	2.67
1994-95	Chicago	22	15	3	5	2.28
1995-96	Chicago	22	17	10	1	2.74
1996-97	Chicago	11	15	6	1	2.69
1996-97	San Jose	3	9	0	1	3.41
1997-98	Dallas	37	12	10	9	1.88
1998-99	Dallas	35	15	9	5	1.99
1999-2000	Dallas	32	21	7	4	2.10
Totals		**308**	**195**	**82**	**49**	**2.47**

that Belfour would be shunted to the background in his moment of success. To a group of reporters crowded around his locker stall, Belfour would later speak of his own personal redemption: "Over and over they said I couldn't do it. Now, finally, people can shut up. They all said I couldn't do this or couldn't do that. Well, I love proving people wrong."

Eddie the Eagle was always something of an eccentric, a moody, brooding presence on game days, with a quick temper that could frequently boil to the surface. "Even though he may be different than most people you play with, he's totally committed to what he has to do," said Stars teammate Joe Nieuwendyk. "A lot of us just let him be and

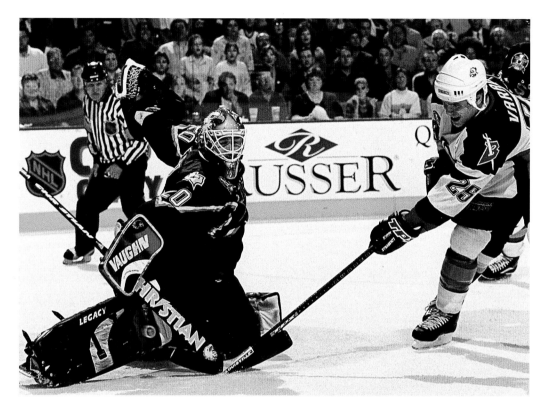

His debt to Tretiak is evident in Belfour's style and his number.

INSIDER**FACT**

Possessing the only two sub-2.00 goals-against average in Stars' team history, Ed Belfour is the NHL's active shutout leader.
The current leaders:

Player	Team	Shutouts
Ed Belfour	Dallas	49
Patrick Roy	Colorado	48
Dominik Hasek	Buffalo	45
Martin Brodeur	New Jersey	42
John Vanbiesbrouck	Philadelphia	38

expect him to be the world-class goalie he is. He's just a fierce competitor. He wants to be the best."

At the age of 20, Belfour was anything but the best. Undrafted by the NHL, Belfour was playing Tier 2 Junior with Winkler of the Manitoba Junior Hockey League. He didn't sign his first pro contract until he was 22, after spending a year at the University of North Dakota. Following a year with Canada's national program, a last-chance outpost for players

At the age of 20, Belfour was anything but the best. Undrafted by the NHL, Belfour was playing Tier 2 Junior with Winkler of the Manitoba Junior Hockey League.

The Eagle usually flies alone even when he wins the Cup.

hanging on by the edge of their fingernails, Blackhawks GM/Coach Mike Keenan rescued him from the scrap-heap and thrust him right into action during the 1990 playoffs, the year Chicago advanced to the semi-finals.

The next year, his rookie NHL season, Belfour won 43 games for the Blackhawks and won the Calder Trophy as rookie of the year. He wore No. 20 to honor Vladislav Tretiak, the Hall of Fame goaltender from Russia who was working as his coach and mentor. Of Tretiak,

Belfour said: "He was great for me, on and off the ice, a true friend who helped my game tremendously."

The hardware kept coming for Belfour - two Vezina Trophies (as the outstanding goalie), four Jennings Trophies (for the best goals-against average) and 300-plus NHL wins and counting. But it was the Stanley Cup in 1999 that finally brought validation to a distinguished, if offbeat, career, even if the attention that morning was elsewhere.

The story Olaf Kolzig tells about his beginnings as a goaltender is oddly charming. As a five-year-old, soon after his parents emigrated to Canada, Kolzig found himself playing for a squirt team in Edmonton, where each player eventually took a turn in goal.

"It was an outdoor rink and I took a shot earlier in that game and the puck stung me because it was really cold out," began Kolzig. "So then there was a breakaway by this kid and I thought, 'I don't want to feel this puck again,' so I turned around and hid right behind the net."

An inauspicious debut to be sure, but eventually Kolzig overcame his fear. Nowadays, the shooters fear him. Born in Johannesburg, South Africa, of German parents (which is why he plays internationally for Germany), Kolzig grew up in Toronto and played both forward and defense in his formative years, which turned him into a good skater, a virtually indispensable skill for a modern-day NHL netminder. Temperamental in his formative years, Kolzig used to smash goalie sticks as a teenager as a means of venting his frustration.

37

O L A F **K O L Z I G**

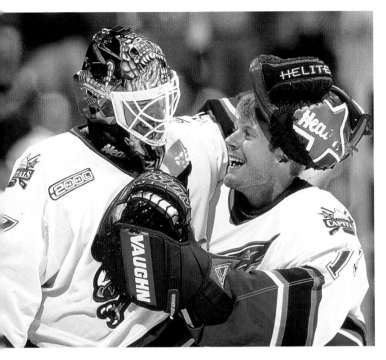

The big guy is not afraid to tell his teammates what to do.

OLAF KOLZIG'S CAREER STATISTICS

Season	Team	W	L	T	SO	GAA
1989-90	Washington	0	2	0	0	6.00
1992-93	Washington	0	0	0	0	6.00
1993-94	Washington	0	3	0	0	5.36
1994-95	Washington	2	8	2	0	2.49
1995-96	Washington	4	8	2	0	3.08
1996-97	Washington	8	15	4	2	2.59
1997-98	Washington	33	18	10	5	2.20
1998-99	Washington	26	31	3	4	2.58
1999-2000	Washington	41	20	11	5	2.24
Totals		**114**	**105**	**32**	**16**	**2.49**

Over time, he came to grips with his profession and understood that not every goal was his fault, or even stoppable. Veteran teammate Joe Reekie says he has never played with a goaltender quite like Kolzig, who delivers a constant stream of direction to his defense corps. "He's not afraid to let you know you made a mistake," said Reekie, a defenseman. "You hear about it."

A No. 1 draft choice in 1989, Kolzig took eight seasons in the Washington Capitals' organization to become an overnight success. After winning just 14 NHL games in his first seven pro seasons, Kolzig won 33 in 1997-98 and then 12 more in the playoffs as the Capitals advanced to the Stanley Cup finals against long odds and the Detroit Red Wings. Getting a taste made Kolzig hungry for post-season success again — and he doesn't mind saying so. "That's part of what makes him great," said Craig Billington, his back-up. "He wants so bad to be the best. He gets hot under the collar but then he lets it go. That's very healthy. They say don't hold anything in, and in that case, Olie is going to live to a very, very ripe old age."

Long before the Legion Of Doom, long before the five consecutive years of 40 goals or more, John LeClair had already had his Andy Warhol moment. Or so it appeared.

LeClair's 15 minutes of fame came in 1993 when he followed a so-so 19-goal regular season by scoring two overtime game winners in the Stanley Cup finals as his Montreal Canadiens won their final championship of the 20th century. For an unheralded second-year pro from nearby St. Albans, Vermont, it didn't get much better than that. Or so it appeared.

Less than two years after LeClair's playoff heroics, the Canadiens traded him and defenseman Eric Desjardins to the Philadelphia Flyers for Mark Recchi. There was little in LeClair's resume — 48 goals in his first 224 NHL games — to suggest he was about to become one of the league's most consistent goal scorers. GM Bobby Clarke notified LeClair that he would audition on Eric Lindros's left wing. Promised the opportunity to line up beside Lindros, LeClair ensured that things worked by scoring 25 goals in the Flyers' remaining 37 games and then following up with three consecutive 50-goal years. Playing with Lindros, LeClair will acknowledge, made

JOHNLECLAIR 10

LeClair's best position: at the net and waiting for the rebound.

JOHN LECLAIR'S CAREER STATISTICS

Season	Team	G	A	Pts.	PIM
1990-91	Montreal	2	5	7	2
1991-92	Montreal	8	11	19	14
1992-93	Montreal	19	25	44	33
1993-94	Montreal	19	24	43	32
1994-95	Montreal	1	4	5	10
1994-95	Philadelphia	25	24	49	20
1995-96	Philadelphia	51	46	97	64
1996-97	Philadelphia	50	47	97	58
1997-98	Philadelphia	51	36	87	32
1998-99	Philadelphia	43	47	90	30
1999-2000	Philadelphia	40	37	77	36
Totals		**309**	**306**	**615**	**331**

a "tremendous difference" in the early stages of his Flyers career.

"Eric is a player who makes the players around him better," said LeClair. What the ultra-modest LeClair doesn't say is that he has maintained his scoring pace, even in Lindros's long absences from the lineup. The quality that sets him apart from the NHL's other exceptional stars is his foot speed — or more precisely, the lack thereof. Others fly, LeClair plods. In LeClair's four years at the University of Vermont, he tried to get his skating up to NHL standards. Nowadays, he will never be confused with Pavel Bure, but his skating is good enough.

"I remember in Montreal, he used to fall down a lot," said defenseman Kevin Haller, a former teammate with the Canadiens. "We used to kid him about that." LeClair's primary skill is his size and strength and he needed time to grow into his body. Once he gets in position in front of the net, defensemen find him to be an immovable block. He has the ability to spin off a check and jockey for position so that if a rebound comes, he is nicely positioned. This is instinct, not luck.

As a player, the Phoenix Coyotes' Jeremy Roenick believes in giving and receiving. For proof, consider the play from the spring of 1999 when Roenick took a punishing, leave-your-feet type of blow from the Dallas Stars captain Derian Hatcher.

The hit fractured Roenick's jaw in three places and left him with a face like Fred Flintstone's — his words — all puffy and discolored.

The fact that Roenick came back from what should have been a season-ending injury within two and a half weeks, so he could play the seventh game of an opening playoff series against the St. Louis Blues, illustrates either a) his fortitude, or b) his recklessness. Was he crazy to do that? "Not in my opinion," answered Roenick. "For anybody who doesn't play sports or doesn't go through pain or know what it's like to be on a team, it may seem crazy, but for me? I just couldn't sit there and watch anymore. I don't have to skate on my

97
JEREMYROENICK

When his jaw was broken, Roenick showed the meaning of sacrifice.

JEREMY ROENICK'S CAREER STATISTICS

Season	Team	G	A	Pts.	PIM
1988-89	Chicago	9	9	8	44
1989-90	Chicago	26	40	66	54
1990-91	Chicago	41	53	94	80
1991-92	Chicago	53	50	103	98
1992-93	Chicago	50	57	107	86
1993-94	Chicago	46	61	107	25
1994-95	Chicago	10	24	34	14
1995-96	Chicago	32	35	67	109
1996-97	Phoenix	29	40	69	115
1997-98	Phoenix	24	32	56	103
1998-99	Phoenix	24	48	72	130
1999-2000	Phoenix	34	44	78	102
Totals		378	493	871	1,020

jaw, I don't have to shoot on my jaw, I don't have to do anything with my jaw on the ice. I just had the attitude, if I broke it again, it'd just be another two months in the summertime when it heals. That didn't bother me. I'm still going to play. Two months is not a big sacrifice to me in relation to what I can gain or obtain."

Once upon a time, Roenick was known as the NHL's most complete player, thanks to three 100-point seasons with the Chicago Blackhawks, in which he was also one of the league's most feared open-ice hitters. Roenick attributes much of his early development as a player to former Blackhawks coach Mike

For JR, the term complete player fits perfectly.

With three 100-point seasons, Jeremy Roenick is the leader in that category among U.S.-born players. The other Americans with more than one 100-point season are Jimmy Carson, Pat LaFontaine and Kevin Stevens. With two 50-goal seasons, Roenick trails only John LeClair, who has three such seasons, and is tied with Kevin Stevens and Coyotes teammate Keith Tkachuk for the American-player lead.

Keenan. "I came into the NHL as a small, light, scared kid," said Roenick. "Keenan turned me into a reckless kamikaze. He scared me into playing that way and I adopted that as my style." Roenick didn't miss much hockey in his first five years as a pro, but then injuries set him back — none more serious than when perennial nemesis Hatcher knocked Roenick out of the 1994-95 playoffs with a knee injury. Questions were asked: Would JR ever be the same player again? The answer: Yes. A bounce-back year in 1999-2000 kept him in

"I don't have to skate on my jaw. I don't have to do anything with my jaw on the ice. If I broke it again, it'd just be another two months when it heals."

A pleasure to play with — or against — him.

company with the league's top scorers. "After I got traded to Phoenix, I tried to settle down with the physical style because I went through some injuries. I tried to change with the times. It's a very defensive system these days. Today, 75 points is what 110 used to be." His Coyotes teammate Mike Sullivan calls Roenick, "one of the most dynamic players I've ever played with. He's exciting to watch, with his speed and his puck-handling ability. His vision on the ice is tremendous."

Roenick believes he's changed with the times. "You don't see the big boys put up the big numbers the way they used to," said Roenick. "I've grown into a different type of player and a different type of person. I know when to pick my spots now. I'm smarter in certain situations." And when his career is over? Roenick wants to be remembered as "a warrior, a winner, a guy that gave everything he had. I want people to say it was a pleasure to play with me — and against me."

The worst year of Mark Recchi's hockey-playing life also coincided with one of the best moments of his personal life — the birth of his daughter, Christina.

It was his final year with the Montreal Canadiens and Recchi, who hadn't missed a game in almost seven seasons, was determined to keep his streak going. He had injuries, he contracted pneumonia, and only when the illness dragged into its third week and showed no signs of improving did he finally stop at 570 games. Within weeks, Recchi found himself traded back to the Philadelphia Flyers, a cause for celebration until he suffered a major concussion that left him confused and incoherent. The after effects lingered — headaches, numbness in his right hand — and only after a summer of healing (and a new five-year, no-trade contract from the Flyers) did he feel right again.

The essence of Recchi's game is his ability to accelerate. In high school, he ran the anchor leg on the 4X100 relay team. A deceptively good athlete, Recchi is a smallish but stocky forward, with an explosive first step. He is also adept at slowing up to convince a defenseman that he has him angled off and zooming past. "From A to B, the explosion, getting out of

8

MARKRECCHI

Recchi is a thinking fan's hockey player.

MARK RECCHI'S CAREER STATISTICS

Season	Team	G	A	Pts.	PIM
1988-89	Pittsburgh	1	1	2	0
1989-90	Pittsburgh	30	37	67	44
1990-91	Pittsburgh	40	73	113	48
1991-92	Pittsburgh	33	37	70	78
1991-92	Philadelphia	10	17	27	18
1992-93	Philadelphia	53	70	123	95
1993-94	Philadelphia	40	67	107	46
1994-95	Philadelphia	2	3	5	12
1994-95	Montreal	14	29	43	16
1995-96	Montreal	28	50	78	69
1996-97	Montreal	34	46	80	58
1997-98	Montreal	32	42	74	51
1998-99	Montreal	12	35	47	28
1998-99	Philadelphia	4	2	6	6
1999-2000	Philadelphia	28	63	91	50
Totals		**361**	**572**	**933**	**619**

the gate, that's my game," he said. Recchi's game evolved in his two Flyers incarnations, something he will freely admit. "I'm more of a complete player now," said Recchi. "Back then (1992, when the Flyers acquired him from Pittsburgh for Rick Tocchet), I was brought in to score and that was my first thought. Now, it's my second thought. The first is defense. I started to think about that my last year here. I had a good talk with Russ Farwell, who was the GM then, and he mentioned Doug Gilmour — how he plays the same way in his own zone as he does in the offensive zone. I really started to work at that. Then, when I got to Montreal, that team needed me to play both ways."

Recchi is also a skilled puckhandler who, more often than not, plays the left point on the power play. Nowadays, only a handful of forwards are deployed there and Recchi needed to convince coach Roger Neilson that he belonged. Recchi energized a low-energy power play, leading the league in both power play assists and points.

That shaved skull and permanent five o'clock shadow gives Pavol Demitra an unnecessarily menacing look, which is somewhat at odds with his real personality.

"He's a quiet, laid-back guy," said Grant Fuhr, his former St. Louis Blues teammate, "but you could have a lot of fun with him."

Once thought of as shy and reticent because of a language barrier, the Slovakia-born Demitra is becoming more open and chatty as his command of English improves. Above all, he is one of the NHL's most unknown, underrated stars, finishing in the top 20 in scoring in successive years. "I would describe him as the most anonymous star in the league," said Fuhr. "People don't realize how skilled Pavol is. He skates really well and shoots the puck well, better than people think. They leaned on him a little bit about playing well in both ends of the ice when he first got there and he's responded. It's made him turn the corner."

Demitra is more assured than when he arrived in St. Louis in a 1996 deal that barely registered a blip on the Transactions radar scale.

38

PAVOLDEMITRA

The Blues darter finds his place and his space.

PAVOL DEMITRA'S CAREER STATISTICS

Season	Team	G	A	Pts.	PIM
1993-94	Ottawa	1	1	2	4
1994-95	Ottawa	4	3	7	0
1995-96	Ottawa	7	10	17	6
1996-97	St. Louis	3	0	3	2
1997-98	St. Louis	22	30	52	22
1998-99	St. Louis	37	52	89	16
1999-2000	St. Louis	28	47	75	8
Totals		**102**	**143**	**245**	**58**

Selected 227th overall by Ottawa in the 1993 entry draft, Demitra joined the Blues in a trade with the Senators for Swedish defenseman Christer Olsson. Mike Keenan, the former Blues GM, made the deal, but it was his successor as coach, Joel Quenneville, who gave Demitra a chance for regular duty. Quick at darting in the holes and a gifted playmaker, Demitra learned to play defense in the Senators' system, thanks mainly to Dave Allison, who coached him in the minors at both Prince Edward Island and Grand Rapids.

More influential even than Allison was Demitra's father. Pavol Sr. was a full-time engineer and a part-time soccer coach in Slovakia, who exerted a strong influence on his son, teaching him about the value of hard work. "He has made me appreciate what I have," said Demitra. "He is where I get my intensity from."

Playing with Slovakian linemates, Michal Handzus and Lubos Bartecko, Demitra was instrumental in the Blues success in 1999-2000. And as his team and his numbers continue to rise, his anonymity is sure to diminish.

The story Mats Sundin tells about his initiation into the hockey-crazed world of Toronto came in the summer of 1994 when, unbeknownst to him, he had been traded by the Quebec Nordiques to the Maple Leafs.

There was Sundin, on wilderness vacation in northern Sweden, fishing rod in hand, when the whirring sounds of a helicopter's rotor broke the silence of the day. The helicopter disgorged a television reporter from Stockholm, sent on a mission to find Mats and chronicle his reaction to the big trade. Life has never been quite the same for the publicity shy Sundin.

The first player chosen in the 1989 entry draft, Sundin left the Nordiques just before they became an NHL powerhouse (and moved on to Colorado). The Maple Leafs grabbed him, in part because 6-foot-5 franchise players do not come available too often. Sundin happened to be working at Borje Salming's hockey school later that summer, so Salming gave him a primer on what to expect from life in Toronto. Much of

13

MATS SUNDIN

Coming to Toronto quickly put privacy in Sundin's past.

MATS SUNDIN'S CAREER STATISTICS

Season	Team	G	A	Pts.	PIM
1990-91	Quebec	23	36	59	58
1991-92	Quebec	33	43	76	103
1992-93	Quebec	47	67	114	96
1993-94	Quebec	32	53	85	60
1994-95	Toronto	23	24	47	14
1995-96	Toronto	33	50	83	46
1996-97	Toronto	41	53	94	59
1997-98	Toronto	33	41	74	49
1998-99	Toronto	31	52	83	58
1999-2000	Toronto	32	41	73	46
Totals		328	460	788	589

Sundin's best hockey has come internationally on behalf of Sweden. Tommy Albelin, a team-mate on the 1996 World Cup and the 1998 Olympic team, says: "He'll do anything to make you feel comfortable. His practice habits are impeccable. He's in great shape. As a player, he may not have the same good hands as Mario Lemieux, but he has the same kind of reach and he plays the same style. Mats is maybe a little faster than Mario was and Mario was maybe better with the puck, but that's the category I would put him in. That's how highly I think of Mats Sundin." Albelin spent a dozen years, trying to wrap up Sundin in front of the net. "Mats weighs like 225 or 230 pounds and he's so strong that it's tough for a defenseman to, first of all, move him. Then, if he gets position on you, what are you going to do? You've got to find a way to get him out of there, but it's tough."

His size and reach put Sundin in a small class of stars.

INSIDER FACT

The first player ever to score four overtime goals in a single season since the NHL introduced OT in the 1983-84 season, Mats Sundin is also the only player in the Toronto Maple Leafs' history to lead the team outright in scoring for six consecutive seasons. Darryl Sittler from 1972-76 led five straight.

Sundin grew up in a suburb of Stockholm and went into the history books as the first European player ever selected first overall in the entry draft. The decision by Quebec was considered something of a gamble, but Sundin conclusively proved that it was the right move by scoring 114 points in his third season with the Nordiques. Sundin has averaged more than a point a game in his first decade in the NHL, but has exceeded the 100-point plateau just the once.

Sundin was the first European selected first in the entry draft. The decision was considered a gamble, but Sundin proved it was the right move by scoring 114 points in his third season.

The Leafs captain had to win the fans over and he did.

There was a time when his name and Jaromir Jagr's were mentioned in the same breath. Physically, the two resemble each other in stature, but Jagr produces more offense. Sundin can be a dominant player because of his size and has the capacity to go in on a rush, fend off the defenseman and — even when it appears as if he is wrapped up — powerfully flick his backhand into the top corner. A second signature move is to slip the puck through a defenseman's skates and then get a shot off while the goaltender is screened.

To acquire Sundin, the Leafs surrendered Wendel Clark, one of their most popular players ever, putting Sundin under enormous pressure. Sundin won the fans over and now he too ranks up there among the most popular Leafs ever. "Playing in Toronto, there is a lot of pressure from the outside," said Sundin, "but the pressure from the surroundings is, I think, a good thing and it makes you play even better."

At age 24, he won the NHL's most valuable player award in 1994, the first European player to do so. Ever since, expectations have weighed heavily on the Detroit Red Wings' Sergei Fedorov.

Fedorov has been one of the NHL's most visible Russian players since he walked away from the Soviet national team at the 1990 Goodwill Games. Fedorov's primary strength is his skating; and more precisely, his capacity to accelerate and then shift gears, without losing control of the puck. "I don't think I've slowed down that much," said Fedorov. "I'm still doing all those things they taught me in Russia years ago. There it was important to be an all-around hockey player, to skate well, to pass well, to battle for the puck. Scoring came last."

So much of what the Red Wings do revolves around team, not individual, goals, something Chris Chelios discovered after he arrived in a trade from Chicago. "Sergei sacrifices a lot of offense for the team and doesn't get the ice time, so that's why he doesn't get a chance to put up the numbers," Chelios said. "Everybody in the league knows he's one of the top players." Fedorov will acknowledge a debt to

91
SERGEIFEDOROV

Everyone knows how good Fedorov is, even if his statistics don't always show it.

SERGI FEDOROV'S CAREER STATISTICS

Season	Team	G	A	Pts.	PIM
1990-91	Detroit	31	48	79	66
1991-92	Detroit	32	54	86	72
1992-93	Detroit	34	53	87	72
1993-94	Detroit	56	64	120	34
1994-95	Detroit	20	30	50	24
1995-96	Detroit	39	68	107	48
1996-97	Detroit	30	33	63	30
1997-98	Detroit	6	11	17	25
1998-99	Detroit	26	37	63	66
1999-2000	Detroit	27	35	62	22
Totals		**301**	**433**	**734**	**459**

former Red Wings teammate Shawn Burr, a fun-loving, outgoing player, who helped him learn the language and adapt to the lifestyle. In his early days of trying to pick up English, Fedorov kept saying to a puzzled Burr: "I need love." Huh? It turns out, what Fedorov really needed was new gloves.

His rapid integration into the U.S. culture convinced Nike to add Fedorov to their stable of all-star athletes in1995. Three years later, in the midst of a season-long contract stalemate with the Red Wings, it was Nike that hosted Fedorov's press conference to announce his Olympic participation. Midway through the Games, Fedorov made headlines by signing a record six-year, $48 million offer sheet with

the Carolina Hurricanes that included an unprecedented $28 million bonus if his team — whatever team he happened to play for — advanced to the third playoff round. The Red Wings gritted their teeth, matched the offer and then — after defending their Stanley Cup championship — grudgingly issued Fedorov his bonus check. Playoffs bring out the best in Fedorov. He scored 20 or more points in four consecutive playoffs, leading the league in postseason scoring in '95.

Over time, people have come to appreciate St. Louis Blues defenseman Al MacInnis for more than just his overpowering slapshot.

He won a Conn Smythe Trophy in 1989 and the Norris Trophy in 1999 and he has gradually evolved into one of the NHL's best all-around defensemen. Still, inevitably, any discussion of MacInnis's impact eventually gets back to The Shot, which — for the better part of two decades now — has been bruising egos and bodies of NHL goaltenders with astonishing regularity.

MacInnis, raised in Port Hood, Nova Scotia as one of eight children, honed his slapshot on summer afternoons by blasting pucks off a plywood sheet into the side of the family barn. Once upon a time, when MacInnis's shot used to veer off in every possible direction, it would be said of him that he couldn't hit the broadside of a barn. That was only a small exaggeration. Eventually he came to control his shot so well that he would aim for the blade of a team-mate's stick in front of the net — and hit it. MacInnis has done little different over the

2

ALMACINNIS

MacInnis is an old-fashioned guy with a stick to match.

AL MacINNIS'S CAREER STATISTICS

Season	Team	G	A	Pts.	PIM
1981-82	Calgary	0	0	0	0
1982-83	Calgary	1	3	4	9
1983-84	Calgary	11	34	45	42
1984-85	Calgary	14	52	66	75
1985-86	Calgary	11	57	68	76
1986-87	Calgary	20	56	76	97
1987-88	Calgary	25	58	83	114
1988-89	Calgary	16	58	74	136
1989-90	Calgary	28	62	90	82
1990-91	Calgary	28	75	103	90
1991-92	Calgary	20	57	77	83
1992-93	Calgary	11	43	54	61
1993-94	Calgary	28	54	82	95
1994-95	St. Louis	8	20	28	43
1995-96	St. Louis	17	44	61	88
1996-97	St. Louis	13	30	43	65
1997-98	St. Louis	19	30	49	80
1998-99	St. Louis	20	42	62	70
1999-2000	St. Louis	11	28	39	34
Totals		**301**	**803**	**1,104**	**1,340**

years to change the mechanics of his shot. Nor is he swayed by all the new technologies of stick manufacturing. Suppliers keep sending MacInnis new product — carbon fiber, graphite, aluminum — in the hope that he will eventually switch from his old-fashioned wooden stick, but he says: "I've tried some of them in practice, but I've never found anything where I can honestly say, 'this is better than what I'm using.'" His stick is short by NHL standards and he brings it straight up and right down in a fast arc. So many NHL players with a high backswing get their shots blocked, but on balance MacInnis gets his off with remarkable regularity. John Davidson, the

MacInnis has been at the top of his game for more than a decade.

INSIDER**FACT**

Since the skills competition became part of the NHL's All-Star weekend, Al MacInnis has been a six-time winnrer of the hardest shot competition.

Year	Winner	Shot
2000	Al MacInnis	100.0
1999	Al MacInnis	98.5
1998	Al MacInnis	100.4
1997	Al MacInnis	98.4
1996	Dave Manson	98.0
1995	No game	
1994	Al Iafrate	102.7
1993	Al Iafrate	105.2
1992	Al MacInnis	93.0
1991	Al MacInnis	94.0
1990	Al Iafrate	96.0

former NHL goaltender and current broadcaster, believes that had MacInnis played in the 1970s, before the innovations in goaltending equipment, he could have perhaps killed a goaltender. Davidson doesn't mean for his observation to be taken metaphorically. "I don't mean they would be in the hospital," said Davidson, "I mean they would be dead."

Even now, MacInnis has a disturbing habit of putting players into the hospital. His shot broke a finger on Chicago Blackhawks goaltender

MacInnis has done little different over the years to change the mechanics of his shot. And he is not swayed by all the new technologies of stick manufacturing.

The Shot: Goalies, teammates and others, beware.

Jocelyn Thibault's catching hand and a bone in Detroit Red Wings goaltender Chris Osgood's blocker hand last season. Two years ago, he fractured teammate Pavol Demitra's jaw with a shot that moved like a knuckleball.

For all the carnage that he's inflicted, the scariest moment came early in his career when Jerry Korab, then with the Buffalo Sabres, slipped and fell in front of MacInnis as he was killing a penalty. With only a split-second to make a decision, MacInnis pulled up and stepped around him. "There's been some very close calls," said MacInnis, "where guys have tried to block a shot, but were in the wrong spot and it just missed them. You say to yourself, 'what was he thinking?' But there's never been a situation like that time with Jerry Korab where a guy was 10 feet in front of me and stumbled and all I could see was his face coming towards me. He actually almost thanked me afterwards, because he knew he was in a bad spot."

His hero growing up in Ontario was the Montreal Canadiens' Larry Robinson, so it was something of a dream come true for defenseman Rob Blake to play with, and then for, Robinson.

They were defense partners with the Los Angeles Kings in the early 1990s and Robinson's primary influence on Blake was in the way he comported himself. As the Kings coach, Robinson demanded a strong work ethic, something Blake never flinched from, even as injuries chipped at his ability to play physically. Indeed, it was two separate surgeries on his shoulders that forced Blake to develop his signature move — a "bee-sting" style of hipchecking that has opposing skaters wary whenever they venture into his patch of ice. "If you hit a guy with your butt against the boards, the whole play is in front of you," said Blake. "I think it's more effective and, truthfully, there's less chance of an injury because you've got more padding back there than anywhere else."

Blake did not play major junior hockey in order to keep himself eligible for a U.S. college scholarship, which he eventually received — to Bowling Green University. The Kings took him 70th overall in the 1990 entry draft and soon discovered they had a potential Norris Trophy

4

ROB BLAKE

When he regained his health, Blake returned to the league's elite.

ROB BLAKE'S CAREER STATISTICS

Season	Team	G	A	Pts.	PIM
1989-90	Los Angeles	0	0	0	4
1990-91	Los Angeles	12	34	46	125
1991-92	Los Angeles	7	13	20	102
1992-93	Los Angeles	16	43	59	152
1993-94	Los Angeles	20	48	68	137
1994-95	Los Angeles	4	7	11	38
1995-96	Los Angeles	1	2	3	8
1996-97	Los Angeles	8	23	31	82
1997-98	Los Angeles	23	27	50	94
1998-99	Los Angeles	12	23	35	128
1999-2000	Los Angeles	18	39	57	112
Totals		**121**	**259**	**380**	**982**

winner. Blake's career went off the rails in a three-year span from 1994 to 1997, when injuries — to his groin, knee, elbow and hand — forced him to miss more games (124) than he played (92). Blake became so frustrated that he considered retiring. Even after he regained his health, Blake found his timing was gone and his confidence ebbed. In September, 1997, he vowed to get his game back, saying: "I don't want to be the guy who was a good player at one time and could have been great, but never lived up to his potential."

That year, Blake exploded back on the NHL scene, finally winning the Norris and earning a place on the first All-Star team. Kings coach Andy Murray says the operative word with Blake right now is "power. Power in terms of the way he hits right through people. Power in terms of his shot — it goes right through the net. Power in terms of skating — he has a powerful stride and can jump up into the play offensively."

Like father, like son? In many ways, much of Brian Leetch's success can be traced to the path that his dad, Jack, forged originally. Jack Leetch was an all-American at Boston College and three decades later, his son followed in his footsteps.

These were the early days of Leetch's hockey career, when the prospect of playing professionally was starting to become a reality. Brian Leetch was, after all, born in Corpus Christi, Texas — his father, a navy man, was stationed there in 1968, the year of Brian's birth. Had the family stayed, Leetch might have become a defensive back at the University of Texas. Instead, the family moved to Connecticut, and dad's new job — managing the first indoor rink in Cheshire, Connecticut — provided the opportunity for lots of ice time. Even so, not a lot of players — make that exactly zero — had advanced to the NHL from Connecticut when Leetch was growing up, so he had absolutely no point of reference. How good would be good enough? Even now, in his second decade in the NHL, it is Leetch's stamina that draws raves from teammates and opponents alike. "He's incredible," said former Rangers teammate Marc Savard. "He plays 30 minutes

2

BRIAN**LEETCH**

The Texas-born, Connecticut-raised NHL star defenseman.

BRIAN LEETCH'S CAREER STATISTICS

Season	Team	G	A	Pts.	PIM
1987-88	NY Rangers	2	12	14	0
1988-89	NY Rangers	23	48	71	50
1989-90	NY Rangers	11	45	56	26
1990-91	NY Rangers	16	72	88	42
1991-92	NY Rangers	22	80	102	26
1992-93	NY Rangers	6	30	36	26
1993-94	NY Rangers	23	56	79	67
1994-95	NY Rangers	9	32	41	18
1995-96	NY Rangers	15	70	85	30
1996-97	NY Rangers	20	58	78	40
1997-98	NY Rangers	17	33	50	32
1998-99	NY Rangers	13	42	55	42
1999-2000	NY Rangers	7	19	26	20
Totals		**184**	**597**	**781**	**419**

a game, but because he's in such good shape, it doesn't bother him. Let's say he's on the ice for a minute 10 seconds or a minute 20 seconds — long shifts — he's able the whole time to be at his top level. There are times when you'd be circling and the puck would be on your stick as soon as you turn."

As a teenager, Leetch enrolled in a prestigious prep school, Avon Old Farms, just outside of Hartford, for his final two high school years and soon began to attract the attention of NHL scouts. A three-points-per-game average — for

a defenseman no less — will do that sometimes. Drafted by the Rangers ninth overall in 1986, he spent a year at Boston College and then joined the United States' 1988 Olympic team. In his first full NHL season, he won the Calder Trophy in 1989. A seminal moment in

Leetch's stamina is legendary, as is his talent.

INSIDER FACT

Owner of 20 regular-season and 15 playoff Ranger club records, Brian Leetch is the highest scoring defenseman in team history and the only player to appear on The Late Show with David Letterman, The Today Show, Late Night with Conan O'Brien and The Howard Stern Show following the team's 1994 Stanley Cup triumph. He is also the only U.S.-born winner of the Conn Smythe Trophy.

Leetch's development came in October 1991, when the Rangers acquired Mark Messier. Fresh off five Stanley Cup championships, Messier recognized immediately that Leetch would have to play a major role if the Rangers were to end their championships jinx. Leetch responded to Messier's words and guidance and took home the 1992 Norris Trophy as the NHL's top defenseman.

Leetch was a convert. Two years later, the Rangers ended their 54-year Stanley Cup

It is Leetch's stamina that draws raves. "He's incredible," said former teammate Marc Savard. "He plays 30 minutes a game, but because he's in such good shape, it doesn't bother him."

When Leetch improved his defensive skills, he won a Norris Trophy.

drought and Leetch won the Conn Smythe Trophy as the playoff's MVP. Never again would Leetch have to listen to that derisive cry of "1940, 1940," signifying the last Rangers' Cup. Quiet and sensitive off the ice, Leetch can be a dominating offensive player on it. He had six years when he produced 75 or more points from the blueline. "He was always an offensive guy when he turned pro," said John Davidson, broadcaster for MSG Network, "but he was criticized for his

defensive play. Now his defensive play has become better than his offensive play. He's much, much stronger than he looks."

The last couple of years have proven more difficult for two reasons — Messier's absence and his attempts to play through injuries. "Talk about grit," continued Davidson. "He took a slapshot from Tampa's Frederik Modin above his glove and played three more shifts — with a fractured arm! He only left the game because he got nauseous on the bench."

The story of Doug Weight Jr., the Edmonton Oilers' stylish center, begins with the story of his father, Doug Weight Sr., a Michigan factory worker who punched out Chryslers for 30 years.

The Weight household revolved around hockey, American-style. Expensive indoor ice time. Rep teams. Tournament play. One year, Doug Sr. coached three teams. His son played for one and practiced with two others. The message came through early on — if Doug Jr. wanted to pursue a career in hockey, he had to work towards it. "He pushed me," said Weight, "and it was good he did."

Weight earned a scholarship at Lake Superior State and then was drafted by the New York Rangers in the second round. Traded to the Oilers for Esa Tikkanen, Weight blossomed in Edmonton. Oilers coach Kevin Lowe played with Weight briefly in New York and believes: "His progression and evolution as a player had a lot to do with the opportunity to play with Craig MacTavish and Kelly Buchberger, two respected leaders. Their presence helped develop his own leadership skills."

On the ice, Weight's primary strengths are his passing and stickhandling. "When Doug's

39

DOUGWEIGHT

For inspiration, Weight only had to look to his dad.

DOUG WEIGHT'S CAREER STATISTICS

Season	Team	G	A	Pts.	PIM
1991-92	NY Rangers	8	22	30	23
1992-93	NY Rangers	15	25	40	55
1992-93	Edmonton	2	6	8	10
1993-94	Edmonton	24	50	74	47
1994-95	Edmonton	7	33	40	69
1995-96	Edmonton	25	79	104	95
1996-97	Edmonton	21	61	82	80
1997-98	Edmonton	26	44	70	69
1998-99	Edmonton	6	31	37	12
1999-2000	Edmonton	21	51	72	54
Totals		**155**	**402**	**557**	**514**

in a groove, he's doing it all," said Lowe. "He's not only passing the puck well, which he does all the time, but he's got a deceptively hard wrist shot, which we're trying to get him to use more often. The other aspect of his game is he competes. He throws bodychecks. He can be gritty."

Weight learned that lesson in his short time playing behind Mark Messier in New York. "You can't be meek and underconfident and be one of the best players in the world," Weight said, "and that's my goal, realistic or not." Weight, a durable and consistent scorer, perennially flirted with the NHL's leader board until the 1996-97 season when injuries — primarily knee

and rib — set him back. He righted himself just before the 1999 playoffs.

"A lot of things happened," said Weight. "First, you get the salary you do. Then Bucky left and I was named captain. You don't want to make excuses, but I was injured a lot. I'm proud of the job I did off the ice but I definitely want to produce more and more in the big games on the ice."

Family was always a big part of Brendan Shanahan's life, so maybe the only regret in a wholly satisfying NHL journey was that his father, Donal, didn't live to see him drink from the Stanley Cup.

That happened for the first time in 1997 and that summer as his Detroit Red Wings team-mates were shuttling the trophy around the world — from Red Deer to Red Square — Shanahan carried the Stanley Cup to his father's grave. A 20-goal scorer for 12 consecutive years, there's a misconception about Shanahan's game. With his size and his strength, people want him to be a reckless hard hitter, a proto-typical power forward. The reality is Shanahan uses his size to fend off the opposition, to get open for a shot. He puts up big power play numbers, but power forward? That term isn't in his vocabulary.

"The people I styled my game after were my three older brothers (Dan, Brian and Shaun)," said Shanahan. "In our family, we played hockey and lacrosse and we tried to play at both ends. Part of the game was hitting and part was scoring and part of the game was defense and part was offense. It was less that we were all-around players and more that we

14

BRENDAN**SHANAHAN**

Despite his size and strength, don't call Shanahan a power forward.

BRENDAN SHANAHAN'S CAREER STATISTICS

Season	Team	G	A	Pts.	PIM
1987-88	New Jersey	7	19	26	131
1988-89	New Jersey	22	28	50	115
1989-90	New Jersey	30	42	72	137
1990-91	New Jersey	29	37	66	141
1991-92	St. Louis	33	36	69	171
1992-93	St. Louis	51	43	94	174
1993-94	St. Louis	52	50	102	211
1994-95	St. Louis	20	21	41	136
1995-96	Hartford	44	34	78	125
1996-97	Hartford	1	0	1	0
1996-97	Detroit	46	41	87	131
1997-98	Detroit	28	29	57	154
1998-99	Detroit	31	27	58	123
1999-2000	Detroit	41	37	78	105
Totals		**435**	**444**	**879**	**1,854**

just didn't stand out in any one area, so we could be given a nickname like offensive guy or defensive guy. I admired certain players in the NHL, but I can't say I patterned myself after any of them. I copied my brothers."

Shanahan broke into the NHL with the New Jersey Devils in 1987, as the second overall pick in the draft. After four years, he signed as a restricted free agent with St. Louis and the cost in compensation was high: Defenseman Scott Stevens. Shanahan rapidly developed into one of St. Louis's most popular players,

fueled by his devilish sense of humor. If you read the Blues player guide in the five years he spent in the organization, Shanahan alternately spent summers running with the bulls in Pamplona; making a cameo appearance in *Forrest Gump*; or acting as a substitute goaltender for Ireland's

There is not a player in the League who has as much fun around the game.

INSIDER FACT

When Brendan Shanahan scored his 400th career goal early in the 1999-2000 season, the milestone meant little to him, the puck even less. Asked what it would mean, he said, "Nothing, really. Just that I've been around and scored some goals." He says he doesn't have a single hockey picture hanging in his house. But, of course, with Shanahan you never are quite sure what's the truth.

World Cup soccer team. These are the products of either, a) a fertile imagination or b) a vivid fantasy life.

Shanahan has a line for all times. Asked about his ageless teammate Igor Larionov, Shanahan said: "He's the Dick Clark of hockey." He once told ESPN's Gary Thorne about his saxophone playing skills, an instrument he claims to play regularly, except on game days. "Why not," asked Thorne? "No sax on game days," deadpanned Shanahan.

If you believe Shanahan, he has run with the bulls in Spain, played World Cup soccer for Ireland and appeared in *Forrest Gump.* Don't even ask about his saxophone playing.

Winning the Cup twice had a bittersweet tinge for Shanahan.

Not everyone appreciated Shanahan's ways. Blues' general manager and coach Mike Keenan traded him to the Whalers for Chris Pronger. After a season in Hartford, Shanahan asked for — and received — a trade to a contender. The Red Wings brought him into Hockeytown on their private plane, with the famous Winged Wheel painted on the side. Like Dorothy, Shanahan knew he wasn't in Kansas (or Connecticut) anymore.

Shanahan likened his first three seasons in Detroit, to a fairy tale — two Stanley Cups and one near miss. It also led to his decision to pass up a chance for unrestricted free agency in 2000 to re-up with the Wings for four more years. "It doesn't matter how much money you make, what the weather is outside or whether you're living on the ocean or living downtown," explained Shanahan, serious for a moment. "The most important thing is how you feel coming away from work every day."

In his hockey-playing life, Val Bure has always hovered in the shadows — of his father, Vladimir, a three-time Olympic swimming star for the Soviet Union; of his brother, Pavel, the high-scoring Russian Rocket; and of his wife, Candace Cameron.

She was a member of the cast of "Full House," a popular television sitcom. It was only after he settled in with Calgary that Bure emerged into the light.

Bure borrowed a few elements of Theo Fleury's game — including his signature move, which involves shooting unexpectedly off his front foot — and made them his own. A smallish forward, Bure discovered that, like Fleury, he could make plays in traffic and use his quickness to dart in and out of the scoring areas. In a breakout 1999-2000 season, Val actually led his brother Pavel in the scoring race for the first two months and kept within striking range for much of the season. "It's a testament to Val that he's come out of the shadows," said Flames teammate Bill Lindsay, who previously played with Pavel in Florida. "He's defined himself as Val Bure, not just Pavel's brother

8

VALERI**BURE**

Valeri Bure's star is coming out of the shadows.

VALERI BURE'S CAREER STATISTICS

Season	Team	G	A	Pts.	PIM
1994-95	Montreal	3	1	4	6
1995-96	Montreal	22	20	42	28
1996-97	Montreal	14	21	35	6
1997-98	Montreal	7	22	29	33
1997-98	Calgary	5	4	9	2
1998-99	Calgary	26	27	53	22
1999-2000	Calgary	35	40	75	50
Totals		**112**	**135**	**247**	**147**

anymore." According to Lindsay, the brothers share two qualities — an underrated work ethic and a hunger to score goals.

Valeri was only 17 when he arrived in North America and needed to find a junior hockey home. He was eventually placed with the Spokane Chiefs of the WHL, in part because his original agent, Ron Salcer, knew the owners, former KC Royals star George Brett and his brother Bob. Motivated to learn English because he wanted to get assimilated as soon as possible, Bure used all kinds of techniques — from watching TV to reading the liner notes of his new CDs. He and Pavel are close and speak by telephone three or four times a week. Their choice of language is a hybrid of Russian and English only they can understand. "When I was playing with Red Army," said Pavel, "the coach (Viktor Tikhonov) used to say, 'His younger brother will be a better player than him.'" Valeri laughs at the compliment. "He always puts me on the same level he is," he said. "Wherever we go, he says, 'Valeri is as good as me.' That makes me feel good."

Watch the New York Rangers' Theoren Fleury play long enough and you begin to take some things for granted. His size, for example. Fleury is 5-6 in a 6-2 hockey universe.

Effectively, Fleury gives away eight inches and an incalculable number of pounds every time he hurls his diminutive body into an opposing defenseman. For Fleury to survive in the rough-and-tumble world of the National Hockey League is remarkable, but for him to star in the league is something else again. "To be an impact player at his size is a marvel," said Dave King, a former coach. "There's nobody else like him."

Nor has there ever been a player quite like Fleury. Historically, other pint-sized players who graduated from junior hockey with monster point totals disappeared into minor-league oblivion or perhaps went to Europe to play a kinder, gentler game. Not Fleury, who embraces the NHL's smash-mouth style.

Growing up, Fleury heard the same veiled criticism at every level, that he was too small to move up. Motivationally, this served him well as he overcame over-long odds, personally and then professionally. His father drank, his mother's health was frequently poor. Once, as

12

THEOREN**FLEURY**

Fleury was too small to play hockey, or so it would seem.

THEOREN FLEURY'S CAREER STATISTICS

Season	Team	G	A	Pts.	PIM
1988-89	Calgary	14	20	34	46
1989-90	Calgary	31	35	66	157
1990-91	Calgary	51	53	104	136
1991-92	Calgary	33	40	73	133
1992-93	Calgary	34	66	100	88
1993-94	Calgary	40	45	85	186
1994-95	Calgary	29	29	58	112
1995-96	Calgary	46	50	96	112
1996-97	Calgary	29	38	67	104
1997-98	Calgary	27	51	78	197
1998-99	Calgary	30	39	69	68
1998-99	Colorado	10	14	24	18
1999-2000	NY Rangers	15	49	64	68
Totals		**389**	**529**	**918**	**1,425**

a 13-year-old, an errant skate blade sliced open an artery in his arm, damaging the nerves so badly that even now he cannot properly do up the cuffs on a dress shirt with his right hand. Fleury's response was to become virtually ambidextrous. He is a lefty in tennis and in ping-pong.

In 1995, he was diagnosed with Crohn's Disease, a chronic and painful irritation of the lower intestine, which periodically flares up to sap him of his strength. Even so, he presses on, his focus on winning another Stanley Cup championship to bookend the one he captured in 1989 as an NHL rookie with the Calgary Flames. "I wasn't the go-to guy then," said Fleury. "Nowadays, I am. The one thing people are going to ask about me is, 'was Theo Fleury a winner?'" The answer, of course, is self-evident.

You can measure a guy's height but you can't measure his heart.

INSIDER**FACT**

The shortest player in the NHL since he turned pro with the Calgary Flames in the 1988-89 season, the 5-6 Theo Fleury is the only player of his diminutive stature ever to score 900 NHL points. An unofficial list of the NHL's all-time great short guys and their listed heights:

Player	Height	Points
Marcel Dionne	5-9	1,771
Denis Savard	5-10	1,338
Dino Ciccarelli	5-10	1,200
Joe Mullen	5-9	1,063
Henri Richard	5-7	1,046
Theo Fleury	5-6	918

"He was, what, an eighth-round pick?" his friend Wayne Gretzky once said. "That's what I always tell kids." While scouts can measure a player's height and his weight and his speed afoot with uncanny precision, it is not so easy to measure some other things. In Fleury's case, the scouts could never quite calculate the size of his heart.

His heart and his resolve are sure to be measured all over again in the coming seasons. After signing a huge contract as a free agent with the New York Rangers before the 1999-2000 season, Fleury faced his biggest on-ice

Theo has "unbelievable spirit," said a former coach. "There's occasionally some showmanship there but 99 percent of the time he's sincere in trying to make something happen."

The entertainer: overcoming obstacles are part of his enjoyment of life.

challenge. He no longer seemed able to score goals as freely as he always had. His first year in New York ended with 15 goals, the fans booing and his team out of the playoffs. Now he must prove again that he belongs and that he deserves the money he's being paid.

"The one thing about Theo is he's got unbelievable spirit," said King. "There's occasionally some showmanship there, but 99 percent of the time, he's sincere in trying to make something happen. He kick-starts guys.

He's a catalyst. He stirs everything up. Some guys don't like that because they don't want things stirred up."

Fleury's answer: Too bad. "There's room in the game for the small player," said Fleury. "Because he's exciting. Because he can get the fans going. Hockey is entertainment. A lot of people don't want to just see the big guys dump it in and hammer each other, they want a little excitement." In effect, that's Fleury exactly — a little excitement.

He has moved alongside his father, Bobby Hull, both 610-goal scorers and tied on the NHL's all-time goal-scoring list. He is the most irreverent player of his generation.

He almost quit hockey at the age of 16 because nobody wanted him. He was an afterthought in the draft, selected as much for his name as for his potential. And yet, when the career of Brett Hull is eventually put into perspective, the player who once answered to the nickname Pickle because of his oddly shaped body — butcher-block wide and a touch bulbous where it tapers at the waist — will go into the history books for one of the most courageous feats in Stanley Cup history. It was in Game 6 of the 1999 finals that Hull scored the game winner — in the third overtime — to secure the final championship of the millennium for his team, the Dallas Stars. Hull played the final game with a torn muscle in his groin and a grade three medial collateral ligament tear in his left knee. So much for the theory that Hull was all hands and no heart.

16

BRETT**HULL**

Hull's biggest goal helped achieve his biggest goal.

BRETT HULL'S CAREER STATISTICS

Season	Team	G	A	Pts.	PIM
1986-87	Calgary	1	0	1	0
1987-88	Calgary	26	24	50	12
1987-88	St. Louis	6	8	14	4
1988-89	St. Louis	41	43	84	33
1989-90	St. Louis	72	41	113	24
1990-91	St. Louis	86	45	131	22
1991-92	St. Louis	70	39	109	48
1992-93	St. Louis	54	47	101	41
1993-94	St. Louis	57	40	97	38
1994-95	St. Louis	29	21	50	10
1995-96	St. Louis	43	40	83	30
1996-97	St. Louis	42	40	82	10
1997-98	St. Louis	27	45	72	26
1998-99	Dallas	32	26	58	30
1999-2000	Dallas	24	35	59	43
Totals		**610**	**494**	**1,104**	**371**

"Winning the Stanley Cup is something I've dreamed about all my life — starting as a kid, growing up in my dad's shadow, working to make a niche for myself." Hull carved that niche, largely in 11 years with the St. Louis Blues, a span in which he led the League in goals for three consecutive years and once produced an 86-goal season, a feat exceeded only by Wayne Gretzky. That year, he won the Hart Trophy as the NHL's MVP.

Hull didn't see much of his father as a teenager — his parents divorced when he

To reach his potential, Hull had to realize he had some.

was 12 — so much of what he inherited was genetic. Bobby Hull was an explosive skater, with the ability to go end-to-end. Brett is less fluid — as a small boy, he preferred to run around the ice in his gym shoes — but instinctively he finds a way of drifting into the open in prime shooting territory. "Bobby would beat you with power, while Brett beats you with deception," said Glenn Hall, a former teammate of Bobby's in Chicago and a former coach of Brett's in Calgary.

"Bobby would beat you with power while Brett beats you with deception," said Hall of Fame goalie Glenn Hall. Brett instinctively finds a way of drifting into the open in prime shooting territory.

He has changed his game in Dallas to fit his team's needs.

Ultimately, the essence of Brett's game was and is his overpowering shot.

John Muckler, the former New York Rangers coach, once said of Hull in his prime: "He has the quickest release I've ever seen, quicker even that Mike Bossy's. The puck hits his stick and it's gone." Did Hull work long hours to develop that skill? No, it was just something he could always do. "Some people were born to be mathematicians," said Hull. "I was born with an ability to shoot a puck. It's all weight transference and timing. You don't have to be strong to have a good shot."

Playing for the Stars, "doesn't allow him to be as creative as he would like to be," said Stars center Joe Nieuwendyk, "but he's still a guy that can put the puck in the net. That's always been his strong suit." Probably always will be, too.

He began to play organized hockey at age eight, only after nagging his parents for permission.

Mom and dad — schoolteachers, born in Barbados — finally relented because they had, after all, allowed Anson Carter's sister Michelle to play soccer, her sport of choice. Fair's fair, right?

For Carter, hockey was always a means to an end. Even before he was dazzling them in Wexford, Ont., he knew he could go a long way in the game he loved. The operative word for Carter is drive. Even as a child, he was extremely goal-oriented. "I've always known what I wanted and I wouldn't let anything stand in my way," said Carter, "not other people's opinions or what they thought about me, friends, potential girlfriends, you name it. I always had a pretty good sense of where I wanted to go." As a teenager, Carter wanted to go to a U.S. college on a hockey scholarship. It's partly why he didn't play major junior hockey. The other part: As a 17-year-old,

33
ANSON**CARTER**

The look of a man who knows what he wants and gets it.

ANSON CARTER'S CAREER STATISTICS

Season	Team	G	A	Pts.	PIM
1996-97	Washington	3	2	5	7
1996-97	Boston	8	5	1	32
1997-98	Boston	16	27	43	31
1998-99	Boston	24	16	40	22
1999-2000	Boston	22	25	47	14
Totals		73	75	148	76

Carter was a 6-1, 140-pound string bean. "My parents would say I was skinny," said Carter, with a laugh. "I thought of myself as being slim. My draft year, I was listed at 170 pounds. I remember a Leaf scout talking to me after I sprained my wrist in the playoffs and he said, 'if you're 170, I'm Don King.'"

Carter spent four years at Michigan State after the Quebec Nordiques grabbed him with their 11th choice, 220th overall, in the 1992 entry draft. He emerged from college as a solid 185-pounder. Upon the completion of his eligibility, Carter asked the prospect-rich Nordiques to trade his rights and they complied. "I was pretty fortunate that Pierre Lacroix was one of those GMs that doesn't bury players," said Carter. After one year in Washington's organization, the Capitals flipped him to the Boston Bruins, where he's been a fixture ever since. As a player, Carter turned himself into a decent skater and looks as if he'll be a consistent 30-goal scorer if he can ever stay healthy. His 1999-2000 season ended prematurely because of surgery on his right wrist. He had been playing on the scoring line and on the checking line. "I honestly believe I can score 40 or 50 goals in this league," said Carter.

There is a long tradition of stars migrating from Broadway to Hollywood, but with Ziggy Palffy, the journey from New York to Los Angeles carried him from the NHL's footlights to its spotlight.

If it weren't for his great nickname — Ziggy Stardust — Palffy would have been, hands down, the NHL's most anonymous star during the time he spent with the struggling New York Islanders.

Physically, Palffy always appeared an odd choice for stardom. He is small at 5-10, 185 pounds and at a time when weight-room body-tone is *de rigueur*, Palffy is anything but buff. His former Islanders roommate Dan Plante once described him as having "no muscle tone at all." Plante went on to add, however: "When it comes to playing hockey, the guy's unbelievable."

The Islanders auditioned him in 1992, but he failed to stick and went home to Slovakia instead of reporting to the minors. The next year, Palffy returned and stuck it out. Learning English via TV sitcoms and compact discs, he needed his strong sense of humor to survive a series of crises on Long Island — in the front office and on the ice. Finally, when the Islanders were jettisoning salaries in the summer of

68
ZIGMUND PALFFY

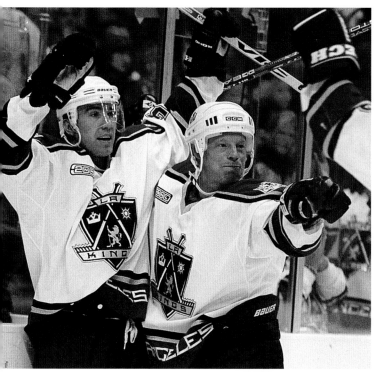

Now that he's with the Kings, Ziggy Stardust is an unknown no longer.

ZIGMUND PALFFY'S CAREER STATISTICS

Season	Team	G	A	Pts.	PIM
1993-94	NY Islanders	0	0	0	0
1994-95	NY Islanders	10	7	17	6
1995-96	NY Islanders	43	44	87	56
1996-97	NY Islanders	48	42	90	43
1997-98	NY Islanders	45	42	87	34
1998-99	NY Islanders	22	28	50	34
1999-2000	Los Angeles	27	39	66	32
Totals		**195**	**202**	**397**	**205**

1999, the Los Angeles Kings won a bidding war with the New York Rangers for Palffy.

Three times a 40-goal scorer and with a reputation as an electrifying offensive player, Palffy was asked to play more of a two-way game by Kings coach Andy Murray. Murray wanted Palffy to know exactly what was — and wasn't — expected of him. He wasn't expected to carry the team offensively. He was expected to be responsible at both ends of the ice. And if his scoring numbers declined, but the Kings made the playoffs? That would be OK.

"The biggest thing with Ziggy is creativity," said Murray. "He can make something out of nothing. He's not the fastest skater and he doesn't have the heaviest shot. He doesn't have all the individual things, but he has the whole package. He's like Paul Kariya in that he sees things other players don't see." For Palffy, the prospect of playing for a winning team would ultimately fill in his resume. Soon after the trade, Palffy was asked to describe his most memorable hockey moment. "Still waiting," he answered.

His favorite movie is *Slapshot*, which is why Keith Tkachuk also answers to Reg. That'd be Reggie Dunlop, the aging Paul Newman character from the cult film that is to hockey players and fans what "The Rocky Horror Picture Show" is to drag queens.

Tkachuk can recite from memory virtually every line of the movie, which is deliciously ironic. Dunlop's goal in *Slapshot* is to save his team from extinction amid an ownership crisis. Talk about life imitating art. In Tkachuk's NHL career thus far, ownership crises have occurred every step of the way, first in Winnipeg, then in Phoenix. It is something he blocks out in an attempt to focus on hockey.

"Keith is a premier power forward in today's game," said Coyotes winger Mike Sullivan. "For a guy as big and as strong as he is, he handles the puck very well. He's a horse down low." Tkachuk arrived in the NHL in 1992, following a year-long stint with the U.S. Olympic hockey team, a raw, hulking kid, with surprisingly soft hands. In his early days, Tkachuk will acknowledge: "At first, I kinda ran around a bit, trying to establish myself and chipping in some goals." Over time, Tkachuk did more than

7

KEITHTKACHUK

Tkachuk is a hulking man with soft hands and an ear for dialogue.

KEITH TKACHUK'S CAREER STATISTICS

Season	Team	G	A	Pts.	PIM
1991-92	Winnipeg	3	5	8	28
1992-93	Winnipeg	28	23	51	201
1993-94	Winnipeg	41	40	81	255
1994-95	Winnipeg	22	29	51	152
1995-96	Winnipeg	50	48	98	156
1996-97	Phoenix	52	34	86	228
1997-98	Phoenix	40	26	66	147
1998-99	Phoenix	36	32	68	151
1999-2000	Phoenix	22	21	43	82
Totals		**294**	**258**	**552**	**1,400**

chip in goals. Twice, he scored 50 in a season and in 1996-97, he became one of only four players in history to join the 50-200 club (50 goals, 200 penalty minutes). A hard-nosed, hard-edged player, Tkachuk was unusually durable in his first five years, considering his style of play, missing only two games. Since then, he's had one serious injury a year for three years running.

"It's a little different for me because I'm the captain and I'm trying to become a leader and help carry this team. Obviously, it's frustrating because I've been hurt a lot. I want to get back to playing 82 games again." The game is so different now that even someone known as Meat (another Tkachuk nickname, after the Tim Robbins character in "Bull Durham") must learn to protect himself better. "There's a lot more hitting than there was 10, 15 years ago," said Tkachuk. "Young guys coming in are bigger and stronger, so you have to be prepared. Injuries happen."

Jeff Friesen learned early about stereotypes and how they can be appallingly incorrect, no matter how you try to overcome them.

In 1994, the highly rated Friesen slipped to 11th spot in the NHL's entry draft, on the theory that he was lazy and had a poor work ethic. Never mind that Friesen's devotion to physical fitness borders on the outright fanatical. Every day in the offseason, he bikes, lifts and skates — and has all the young (and some not so young) San Jose Sharks tagging along. After six NHL seasons and more than 400 games, Friesen is currently the highest-scoring player from his draft class. He has more points than Radek Bonk or Ryan Smyth or Jeff O'Neill and yet, he's still a work in progress.

"You have to be in that dressing room to really know him," said Sharks coach Darryl Sutter, "but of all the kids in there his age or younger, there's no question about who is the leader, the go-to guy. He sets an example, in the room and on the ice." As a player, Friesen relies

JEFFFRIESEN

Friesen is working hard to reach his own goals.

JEFF **FRIESEN'S** CAREER **STATISTICS**

Season	Team	G	A	Pts.	PIM
1994-95	San Jose	15	10	25	14
1995-96	San Jose	15	31	46	42
1996-97	San Jose	28	34	62	75
1997-98	San Jose	31	32	63	40
1998-99	San Jose	22	35	57	42
1999-2000	San Jose	26	35	61	47
Totals		**137**	**177**	**314**	**260**

on his exceptional speed and Pavel Bure-like acceleration. In his early years, he could catch teams by surprise by skating away from the defenseman. Nowadays, teams know that Friesen can kill you if he gets a step on you. Does he have the capacity to be an elite player? "It depends if he can score 40 goals," said Sutter. "He plays a lot of minutes, he plays hurt, he plays every game. I don't think you're going to see him at his best for another three or four years — and he's improved tremendously every year since I've been here."

Friesen perennially lands in the top 50 of NHL scorers, but thinks he can do more. Much more. "With a long NHL year, you need to stay with it and be consistent," said Friesen. "I feel I can get into that 30-, 35-, 40-goal range and to that 80-point plateau. That's something I have to work hard to do." Said Paul Baxter, the Sharks assistant coach: "Jeff has a Gretzky-like quality; he's the type of player that wants to be the best in the League." Not a bad compliment considering what they were saying about Friesen early in his career.

At 18, they were calling him *The Next One*, even before Eric Lindros had played his first National Hockey League game. For the next decade, Lindros labored under the burden of high, unyielding expectations, brought on by that veiled comparison to Wayne Gretzky.

It's funny because Lindros was always more of a Mark Messier type — a strapping 6-4 giant, with soft hands and a big heart, who gets himself into trouble by trying to do the right thing. Lindros was trying to do the right thing when Philadelphia Flyers general manager Bobby Clarke named him captain of Canada's 1998 Olympic team ahead of more logical choices such as Gretzky or Steve Yzerman. He was trying to do the right thing in the spring of 1998 when he came back for the playoffs after missing 18 games with a concussion, but was never really right. The next spring, he was trying to do the right thing again when, following a game against the Nashville Predators, he ignored the symptoms of a

88
ERICLINDROS

The disturbances to mind and body have long affected this unique talent.

ERIC LINDROS'S CAREER STATISTICS

Season	Team	G	A	Pts.	PIM
1992-93	Philadelphia	41	34	75	147
1993-94	Philadelphia	44	53	97	103
1994-95	Philadelphia	29	41	70	60
1995-96	Philadelphia	47	68	15	163
1996-97	Philadelphia	32	47	79	136
1997-98	Philadelphia	30	41	71	134
1998-99	Philadelphia	40	53	93	120
1999-2000	Philadelphia	27	32	59	83
Totals		**290**	**369**	**659**	**946**

collapsed lung until his roommate Keith Jones found him slumped in a bathtub, nearly bleeding to death. In 2000, a similar thing. He tried to play through a concussion, his fourth, by popping Advil by the score to diminish the symptoms and the pain.

Lindros is always trying and never living up to the expectations — of his nickname, of his boss, of a demanding sporting public. Never one to soft-pedal an issue, Clarke challenged Lindros during their '98 contract negotiations to do more of everything — score, lead, win. He wanted Lindros to grow up. If he wanted to be hockey's highest-paid player, he better do something to earn the pay. It all boiled over last spring when Lindros squawked about the support and medical care he was receiving from the Flyers' organization. Clarke stripped Lindros of the Flyers' captaincy. The war of words between the two escalated until it became clear the pair had reached what seemed the point of no return.

Lindros has never shied away from the physical part of the game.

INSIDER FACT

Despite his injury-disrupted career, Eric Lindros has 659 points in 489 career games, a points per game average of 1.347. Only Mario Lemieux (2.005), Wayne Gretzky (1.921), Mike Bossy (1.497) and Bobby Orr (1.393) have better marks for players with 500 or more points.

There was nothing wrong with Lindros that good health and a Stanley Cup ring wouldn't cure. On a points-per-game basis, Lindros averages around 1.40, the fourth-highest mark in league history. The three players above him — Mario Lemieux, Wayne Gretzky and Mike Bossy — all had the luxury of playing in an era when scoring was far more common. Oilers defenseman Igor Ulanov, who had some epic battles with Lindros in playoffs past, holds his opponent in high regard.

On a points-per-game basis, Lindros averages around 1.40, fourth in history. The three players above him — Mario Lemieux, Wayne Gretzky and Mike Bossy — all played when scoring was more common.

When asked, Lindros refuses to speculate on 'what if.'

"Obviously, Eric's a big strong player with a lot of talent," said Ulanov. "He's got a lot of speed and very good hands, so it's not that easy to play against him. He's very physical as well, so you have to keep your head up all the time. To play successfully against him, you just have to stay in his face, be close to him all the time and make sure he doesn't have much time with the puck."

Coach Roger Neilson, always one of Lindros's biggest boosters, compared Lindros to Darryl Sittler, "who was my first captain with the Toronto Maple Leafs and was always the hardest working guy at every practice. Eric's the same way." Lindros was once asked: Would it have been easier to play 30 years ago, when his odds were dramatically better to win a championship than they are today? "I can't answer that," replied Lindros. "It's not something that's going to happen, so it doesn't do me any good to think about the possibility."

VINCENT LECAVALIER

SCOTT GOMEZ

PATRIK ELIAS

ROBERTO LUONGO

TOM POTI

JAROME IGINLA

JOE THORNTON

CHRIS DRURY

MILAN HEJDUK

MARIAN HOSSA

SERGEI GONCHAR

SAMI KAPENEN

DAVID LEGWAND

JOSE THEODORE

2

TOMORROW'S STARS

In the era of an 18-year-old draft, there is considerable uncertainty involved in identifying hockey talent before it fully develops and matures. And yet, each year the NHL welcomes a steady stream of precocious youngsters, all with the potential and promise of greatness. Some will meet those expectations and others will level off. *Tomorrow's Stars* will introduce you to 14 players on the cusp of stardom, whose talents are ready to mature and blossom.

His first club owner called him "the Michael Jordan of hockey" on Vincent Lecavalier's draft day and ever since the new owners of the Tampa Bay Lightning have tried to lessen the pressure.

They believe their rangy young center will evolve into one of the game's premier players. The proof: When Chris Gratton was traded, the Lightning made Lecavalier, at 19, the youngest team captain in NHL history. Always a tireless worker, even with his high skill level, Lecavalier immediately took his new responsibilities to heart. "It's my duty, now that I'm captain, to work as hard as I can and to help this team win," Lecavalier said. "I want us to make the playoffs and I want us to become one of the best teams in the League. Winning is all that matters." Tall and strong, Lecavalier is a crafty playmaker, with great balance and agility. Coach Steve Ludzik doesn't go overboard in praising Lecavalier, but suggests his second-season progress was nothing short of astonishing. "I don't think I've ever seen a player develop as much and as quickly from the start of the season as Vinny has," said Ludzik.

VINCENT LECAVALIER'S CAREER STATISTICS

Season	Team	G	A	Pts.	PIM
1998-99	Tampa Bay	13	15	28	23
1999-2000	Tampa Bay	25	42	67	43
Totals		38	57	95	66

4
VINCENTLECAVALIER

In the beginning, reporters flocked to the New Jersey Devils' Scott Gomez because of his compelling story — the first Hispanic player ever to play in the NHL.

Never mind that Gomez cut his hockey-playing teeth in Anchorage, Alaska, where his parents had settled so father Carlos could work on the

SCOTT GOMEZ'S CAREER STATISTICS

Season	Team	G	A	Pts.	PIM
1999-2000	New Jersey	19	51	70	78

Alaskan pipeline. "Some people think I just came from Tijuana last year and learned how to play hockey," said Gomez, with a laugh. "Or that I lived in an igloo." Eventually, reporters began flocking to Gomez because of what he was doing on the ice. Gomez won the NHL's rookie scoring crown, with a game that revolves around playmaking. "On the ice, he always has a plan," said Devils defenseman Scott Stevens. "A lot of young players don't think until they get the puck. He knows what he's going to do with the puck before he gets it." Devils general manager Lou Lamoriello describes this as Gomez's "god-given ability to see plays prior to those plays developing. He makes other players better."

23

SCOTTGOMEZ

Patrik Elias is a funny guy on the sometimes far-too-serious New Jersey Devils, someone who appreciates lowbrow humor and doesn't mind owning up to it.

Example: In the 1999-2000 season, Elias found himself unexpectedly squaring off to fight Detroit's Slava Kozlov. They are two of the NHL's most committed pacifists, which made the exchange all the more cartoonish. Afterwards, Elias entertained reporters by shadow-boxing as he quipped: "I've got to ice

PATRIK ELIAS'S CAREER STATISTICS

Season	Team	G	A	Pts.	PIM
1995-96	New Jersey	0	0	0	0
1996-97	New Jersey	2	3	5	2
1997-98	New Jersey	18	19	37	28
1998-99	New Jersey	17	33	50	34
1999-2000	New Jersey	35	37	72	58
Totals		72	92	164	122

my hands now ... I really unleashed these babies." The only thing dumb and dumber than Elias's punch lines may be the fact that so many NHL teams ignored him in his 1994 draft year — or until the Devils grabbed him 51st overall. Devils assistant coach Slava Fetisov likens Elias to former Russian star Sergei Makarov, a squat, wide-bodied forward, who was strong on the puck and slick around the net. Unlike Makarov, who was moody and sullen, Elias is right in the middle of everything that goes on in the Devils' dressing room. He is a multi-dimensional player, with the talent to produce offense and the mindset to muck. "This is a fun game to play," said Elias.

26
PATRIK ELIAS

No goaltender has ever been selected as high in the entry draft as the New York Islanders' Robert Luongo, who went fourth overall in 1997.

"There was a reason for that too," said Islanders general manager Mike Milbury. "In time, we believe he can be an elite-level goalie." Luongo, who is trilingual (he speaks French, English and Italian) began his playing career as an extremely average forward, but at age 11, when he didn't make a house-league team in St.-Leonard, Quebec, he switched to goal — and the rest is history. One of the many Quebec-born goalies influenced by Patrick Roy, Luongo is a classic butterfly-style goaltender, but uses his 6-3 frame and an upright stance to block the top corners as well. More importantly, he is mentally resilient and doesn't allow bad goals to deflate him. "Really, nothing seems to faze him," said Milbury. The Islanders gave him a 24-game cameo in the 1999-2000 season before returning him to the minors. "There's pressure in being drafted so high, but if you're going to play, you're going to have to deal with pressure. And," concludes Luongo, "I love pressure."

ROBERTO LUONGO'S CAREER STATISTICS

Season	Team	W	L	T	SO	GAA
1999-2000	NY Islanders	7	14	1	1	3.25

ROBERTOLUONGO

1

On the day he turned 23, his Edmonton Oilers teammates presented defenseman Tom Poti with a cake. Chocolate. Poti thanked them and made sure everybody — except himself — received a piece.

Poti cannot eat chocolate or nuts or use alcohol. Food allergies, diagnosed when he was a boy, mean if he eats something on his disapproved list, his throat closes. Poti travels with a full complement of snacks, including bread, in his carry-on. In his rookie year, he would enter hotel kitchens to discuss the menu. Now, the

TOM POTI'S CAREER STATISTICS

Season	Team	G	A	Pts.	PIM
1998-99	Edmonton	5	16	21	42
1999-2000	Edmonton	9	26	35	65
Totals		14	42	56	107

team outlines what can and cannot be served. A quintessential rushing defenseman, Poti played at Boston University and was not drafted until the fourth round because of his scarecrow-thin, 175-pound frame. Teams worried that his allergies could not be controlled. The first time Oilers GM Glen Sather saw Poti at the 1996 draft, he looked nothing like a modern-day player. "I looked at our scouts and was thinking, 'you've got to be kidding'," said Sather. Now he's up to 215 and pleases the Oilers with his puck-handling skills and passing ability.

5
TOMPOTI

In Nigeria, the name Iginla translates into Big Tree, which is an apt way of describing the Calgary Flames right winger Jarome Iginla.

Apart from his omnipresent smile, Iginla's most visible characteristic is his sturdiness through the trunk. In Iginla's first year, when he finished second to Bryan Berard in the Calder Trophy race, the puck seemed to follow him, which indicates good hockey sense. "Iggy's starting to believe he can be a good player," says future Hall of Fame goaltender Grant

Fuhr, "and that's half the battle. You gotta believe in yourself before good things start to happen — and he does now."

Iginla's father, Elvis, is a black Nigerian who split up with his white Canadian mother, Susan, when Jarome was just two. Growing up in Edmonton, Iginla's hero was Fuhr, who was also of a mixed racial background. "People would ask me, 'why don't you play basketball or football?' and I'd point to Grant and say, 'he's black and playing hockey, so I can too.' I didn't think being black was a barrier to playing in the NHL." Nor has it been.

JAROME IGINLA'S CAREER STATISTICS

Season	Team	G	A	Pts.	PIM
1996-97	Calgary	21	29	50	37
1997-98	Calgary	13	19	32	29
1998-99	Calgary	28	23	51	58
1999-2000	Calgary	29	34	63	26
Totals		91	105	196	150

JAROMEIGINLA

12

By age 18, he was already 6-4, 225, with the wingspan of a condor. Rationally, intuitively, the Boston Bruins knew that Joe Thornton needed time to grow into his body.

The first player chosen in the 1997 entry draft, Thornton contributed all of seven points in 55 games in his rookie season and people were prepared to say the Bruins goofed. Two seasons later, Thornton finished with 60 points to lead

JOE THORNTON'S CAREER STATISTICS

Season	Team	G	A	Pts.	PIM
1997-98	Boston	3	4	7	19
1998-99	Boston	16	25	41	69
1999-2000	Boston	23	37	60	82
Totals		**42**	**66**	**108**	**170**

the team. "When Joe first came, the guys in the dressing room knew he wasn't going to have the impact right away," said teammate Anson Carter. "The skills were there, but just mentally, he was still young. In your first year, it doesn't matter if you're 18 or 22, you're still overwhelmed." Injuries to Carter and Jason Allison made Thornton step up. "I know I have to do that to help this team win," said Thornton. He took virtually all of the important faceoffs and evolved into the go-to player. "Now, he knows he can make an impact on any given night," said Carter. "He's strong along the wall and he's developing a mean streak, too, and that's giving him a lot more room out there on the ice."

6
JOE THORNTON

For Chris Drury, the Colorado Avalanche forward, there was always the question of whether he had peaked too early. In 1989, at the age 13, the Trumbull, Connecticut, native pitched the U.S. to the Little League World Series title.

For some, that would be enough. But for Drury? No. "I think a good way to describe it is, you get greedy. I was lucky enough to win

CHRIS DRURY'S CAREER STATISTICS

Season	Team	G	A	Pts.	PIM
1998-99	Colorado	20	24	44	62
1999-2000	Colorado	20	47	67	42
Totals		40	71	111	104

championships at such a young age, but it's just made me want to get more and more, no matter what sport it is." Only a fourth-round pick of the Colorado Avalanche in 1994, Drury won an NCAA championship at Boston College and took home the 1998 Hobey Baker award. Drury followed up by winning the Calder Trophy as the League's rookie of the year, and then came through with a solid second season. "When you win a championship, that first hour after a game's decided, you're on top of the world. Then, as you take some time and distance yourself from it, you develop a good sense of accomplishment. For me, once it's over and two or three days go by, I'm ready to move."

37

CHRISDRURY

His entry to the world stage came in Nagano, when he played on the fourth line of a Czech Republic team that boasted Jaromir Jagr and Dominik Hasek and won the gold medal.

Soon afterwards, Milan Hejduk would star as an NHL rookie, playing alongside another well-known Olympian, Joe Sakic. Much of Hejduk's early notoriety came as a result of his association with hockey's rich and famous. But the reality is Hejduk has evolved into a great player in his own right. "Milan finds the puck," said Sakic. "He doesn't need a lot of room to get the shot off. He doesn't lean into his shot, he kind of scoops it. It's quick and accurate." Hejduk stayed home until he matured physically. "I started in the Czech League when I was 17 and I played five years there," said Hejduk. "I think these years helped me." Hejduk didn't get to the NHL until he turned 23 and it was only after he made the Avalanche out of training camp that teammates and opponents took notice. Coach Bob Hartley describes him as "one of the NHL's smartest hockey players in all three zones."

MILAN HEJDUK'S CAREER STATISTICS

Season	Team	G	A	Pts.	PIM
1998-99	Colorado	14	34	48	26
1999-2000	Colorado	36	36	72	16
Totals		50	70	120	42

23
MILANHEJDUK

The most difficult moment of Marian Hossa's hockey life came late last season when, following through on a slapshot, he inadvertently struck the Leafs' Bryan Berard in the eye.

All the things that Hossa, the Ottawa Senators winger, had gone through up until that point — emigrating from Slovakia, recovering from a major knee reconstruction as a junior — paled in comparison to that helpless feeling: knowing Berard had a serious injury, not being able to offer anything but heartfelt apologies. Hossa is part of a new breed of European who

MARIAN HOSSA'S CAREER STATISTICS

Season	Team	G	A	Pts.	PIM
1997-98	Ottawa	0	1	1	0
1998-99	Ottawa	15	15	30	37
1999-2000	Ottawa	29	27	56	32
Totals		44	43	87	69

began his NHL apprenticeship in major junior and adapted to the language and the style. It was Hossa's rehab from the knee injury that, according to Coach Jacques Martin, addressed the only perceived weakness in his game, skating. "When he came back, he was a different player," said Martin. "He had really improved his speed and his skating." The Senators stepped up Hossa's offensive role in his second year and as a result he found himself facing more aggressive defense. "They play much tighter on me and there's not much room," said Hossa, "but you can't let that frustrate you."

18

MARIANHOSSA

Of the five first-round draft choices the Washington Capitals received from the St. Louis Blues as compensation for signing free-agent defenseman Scott Stevens back in 1990, only one made an impact — Sergei Gonchar.

The underrated, largely unknown Gonchar has quietly evolved into one of the League's premier offensive defensemen.

He can run hot and cold like a tap. Cold: No goals in the first 19 games of the 1999-2000 season. Hot: 14 goals in a 27-game span

SERGEI GONCHAR'S CAREER STATISTICS

Season	Team	G	A	Pts.	PIM
1994-95	Washington	2	5	7	22
1995-96	Washington	15	26	41	60
1996-97	Washington	13	17	30	36
1997-98	Washington	5	16	21	66
1998-99	Washington	21	10	31	57
1999-2000	Washington	18	36	54	52
Totals		74	110	184	293

thereafter. The year before, Gonchar missed the start of the season because of a contract dispute but scored 21 goals in the final 40 games to lead NHL defensemen. Not only does Gonchar possess a great shot, he also has good instincts for jumping into the opening — either as a trailer on the rush or by sneaking in from the point. Capitals coach Ron Wilson calls this Gonchar's "stealth mode," noting that opponents frequently lose track of him. "All of a sudden, Sergei materializes to score a goal from in front of the net and you ask, 'Where did he come from?'"

55
SERGEIGONCHAR

Considering he is one of the NHL's pure young snipers, it may be hard to believe that Sami Kapanen began his hockey career as a goaltender.

His father, Hannu, played in the Finnish Elite League and is now one of the country's premier coaches. His brother, Kimmo, holds up the family tradition, playing goal for Sami's former team, Kalpa Kuopio. Kapanen is something of a late bloomer, drafted in 1995 by the Hartford Whalers as a 22-year-old. His breakthrough year came when the Whalers shifted to Carolina for the 1997-98 season. Kapanen scored 50 goals in his first two seasons in Carolina. The essence of his game is speed, and Kapanen won the fastest skater contest at the 2000 All-Star Game. "Sami uses his speed to get himself into the position to shoot the puck," said Hurricanes center Ron Francis. "Then, with the shot he has, that allows him to score a lot of goals. He's still young and learning, but when he puts it all together, he has the potential to have some really big seasons."

SAMI KAPANEN'S CAREER STATISTICS

Season	Team	G	A	Pts.	PIM
1995-96	Hartford	5	4	9	6
1996-97	Hartford	13	12	25	2
1997-98	Carolina	26	37	63	16
1998-99	Carolina	24	35	59	10
1999-2000	Carolina	24	24	48	12
Totals		92	112	204	46

24

SAMI KAPANEN

David Legwand is developing in football country — Nashville, Tennessee — where fans expect players drafted second overall to be 23 and able to make an impact right away.

How do you ensure that expectations are not unrealistic for this teenager? "We explain that playing in the NHL as a 19-year-old is the same as going from high school straight to

DAVID LEGWAND'S CAREER STATISTICS					
Season	Team	G	A	Pts.	PIM
1998-99	Nashville	0	0	0	0
1999-2000	Nashville	13	15	28	30
Totals		13	15	28	30

the NFL," said Predators coach Barry Trotz. Legwand is a dynamic skater, with the ability to beat a defenseman to the outside. He is patterning his game after Peter Forsberg's. Legwand's first — and most important — lesson upon arriving in the pros: "Night in and night out, it's a hockey game in the NHL. That's the thing you have to learn — to compete every night. Consistency is a big thing in this league." The Predators eased him in, enabling him to get his feet wet. Much bigger things are expected and that's okay because he expects big things of himself as well. "It's a big-time challenge here," he said, "but that's what I want. You've got to take the responsibility upon yourself to do the job."

11
DAVID LEGWAND

Before Extreme Sports became a staple on cable television, Jose Theodore was a devotee. As a 12-year-old, Theodore broke his leg snowboarding.

He picked up assorted scrapes and bruises skateboarding and riding his dirt bike. Don't even ask about jumping off a 20-foot ledge into a lake near his hometown of St. Bruno, Quebec. All that living on the edge is in his past, but it goes a long way to explaining why Theodore isn't rattled by breaking in as a

JOSE THEODORE'S CAREER STATISTICS

Season	Team	W	L	T	SO	GAA
1995-96	Montreal	0	0	0	0	6.67
1996-97	Montreal	5	6	2	0	3.87
1998-99	Montreal	4	12	0	1	3.29
1999-2000	Montreal	12	13	2	5	2.10
Totals		21	31	4	6	2.86

goaltender in Montreal. The ghost of Patrick Roy hovers over every young Quebec goaltender and it is omnipresent when that young goaltender plays for Les Habitants. The Canadiens promoted Theodore to the NHL at 19 and for two years he made cameo appearances, none especially memorable. The breakthrough came mid-season in 1999-2000 when the Canadiens, on the playoff ropes, gave him a stretch of games and Theodore played astonishingly well. "He's worked hard to learn from his mistakes," assessed Canadiens goalie coach Roland Melanson. Added Theodore: "I had no doubt that I belong here, but this year was important for me to show everyone that I could step in."

JOSETHEODORE

60

HENRIK SEDIN

DANIEL SEDIN

PATRIK STEFAN

TIM CONNOLLY

ROBYN REGEHR

BRAD STUART

JASON SPEZZA

JAY BOUWMEESTER

3

STARSONTHEHORIZON

Every sports fan has a prediction. Who is going to win? Who is going to be a star? As the NHL enters the new century, with high hopes and broad expectations, watch for these eight players to take center stage and earn their places in the spotlight. They have the capacity to evolve into the next generation of greats and the raw materials to provide memories and stories for years to come. And if they happen to win the MVP or the Stanley Cup, you can say you knew them when.

HENRIK SEDIN

DANIEL SEDIN

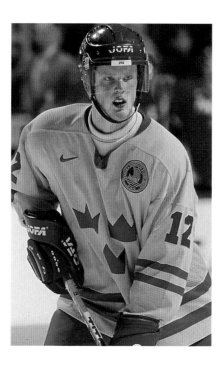

They have similar red, crew cut hair and a similar Scandinavian reticence. One, Henrik, plays center and is a bit taller than the other, Daniel, the right winger. For a time, the only way to tell them apart was to say cheese and ask them to smile. There, Henrik is the one with the chipped right tooth, the result of a high stick he absorbed in a Swedish Elite League game two years ago.

That was the year the Sedin twins were named co-MVPs of their league, an unprecedented achievement for players so young. "That's impossible," said Vancouver Canucks general manager Brian Burke. "It was an amazing feat — to do that at age 17, in an outstanding League, where they were playing against men."

Burke thought so much of the twins that he engineered a complicated series of draft-day trades in 1999 that gave him the second and third overall choices — which he promptly used to grab both players. "We felt there was a chemistry there — that the sum of the two was greater than the individual parts broken down," said Burke. He quickly signed the Sedins, but gave them permission to play one more season in the Swedish Elite League. On the ice, Henrik — older by six minutes — is a better two-way player, with natural offensive vision and good hockey sense. He is more reliable defensively. Daniel is the sniper, a natural-born finisher, with the ability to score highlight-film goals.

They were born in Ornskoldsvik, Sweden, a city of 58,000 near the Arctic Circle that has produced Peter Forsberg, Markus Naslund and Niklas Sundstrom. The Canucks' Naslund, who played with the Sedins at the world championship, said: "They have the talent to become star players in the NHL. The future looks bright for the Canucks."

PATRIK STEFAN

The day may come when not every query relating to Patrik Stefan begins with his head. Three concussions in his draft year made some teams view him as damaged goods before the Atlanta Thrashers made him the first pick in 1999. "I spent so much time watching him and being with him, I feel like his stepfather," said Thrashers GM Don Waddell. "Whatever risks there are because of his concussions, we feel they were worth it because of his potential."

The second player from the Czech Republic to go No. 1 overall, Stefan had joined the Long Beach Ice Dogs as a teenager in the hopes of fast-tracking his career. Stefan uses his long reach as he carries the puck. He is a crisp, accurate passer, and a better one-on-one player than many believe. John Van Boxmeer, who coached him in Long Beach, says: "There are people who compare him to Paul Kariya or Jaromir Jagr. I don't think those are unrealistic."

TIM CONNOLLY

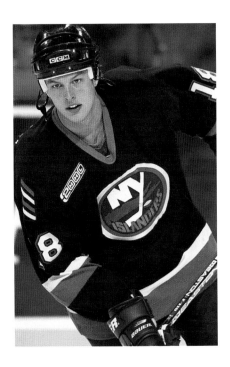

He was the youngest player in the NHL during the 1999 - 2000 season and didn't celebrate his 19th birthday until three weeks after the New York Islanders' year ended. By then, much of the fear (was Tim Connolly ready?) had subsided. From Baldwinsville, N.Y., a suburb of Syracuse, Connolly was the fifth player chosen in the 1999 entry draft and general manager Mike Milbury figures he got a steal: "We think Connolly has a chance to be the best player in the draft." An excellent stickhandler, with a powerful shot, some believe Connolly's size and a maturity beyond his years suggest he could evolve into a Steve Yzerman-type. Islanders player personnel director Gordie Clark said: "He's way ahead of where we thought he would be." That Connolly was so good so soon is even more remarkable considering he missed the final third of his last junior year, recovering from a broken leg.

ROBYNREGEHR

In July of 1999, Robyn Regehr of the Calgary Flames broke both legs in a terrifying head-on traffic collision that put his career in jeopardy. Regehr's first thoughts were survival. Soon the focus on hockey returned. His legs healed quickly, so in two months time he was back skating. After four months, he was playing regularly on defense in the NHL. "Sometimes, I think about the accident when I'm wearing shorts and can see the scars on my legs," said Regehr, "but it's not in the forefront of my mind any longer." An extraordinary individual on many levels — Regehr was born in Brazil and grew up in Indonesia, the son of Mennonite missionaries. He didn't play hockey until he was eight. At 19, he became the youngest nominee for the Masterton Trophy, awarded for perseverance, dedication and sportsmanship.

BRADSTUART

Apart from his powerful skating stride, his excellent slapshot and his underrated aggressiveness, the quality that sets San Jose Sharks defenseman Brad Stuart apart is that he was born with only one kidney. It didn't deter the Sharks from grabbing him with the third overall pick in the 1998 entry draft and it didn't stop Stuart from registering a wholly impressive first season, playing alongside perennial all-star Gary Suter. The year before Stuart signed, the Sharks sent Suter, then on injured reserve, to watch Stuart. "It was like a cat toying with a mouse," said Suter. Stuart said the most important lesson he learned in his first year was preparation. "It's so important to be ready to play when the puck's dropped — and how easy it is to tell when you're not ready."

JASONSPEZZA

No less a hockey authority than Don Cherry believes Jason Spezza will become the NHL's next impact player. Spezza plays for Cherry's junior team, the Mississauga IceDogs, and his much-anticipated coming-out party will occur at the 2001 NHL entry draft. At 16, Spezza played for Canada's world junior team and in the eyes of Minnesota Wild scout Tom Thompson, he is an exceptional prospect. "He's very smart," said Thompson, "and he has excellent hands. Besides seeing the plays, he can make them, too. To me, the most underrated skill in hockey isn't making a pass, it is receiving a pass — and he can do that really well." Spezza understands his gifts. "I set high goals for myself," he said. "I want to be the best hockey player I can be. I don't want to waste my talent, I want to get the most out of it."

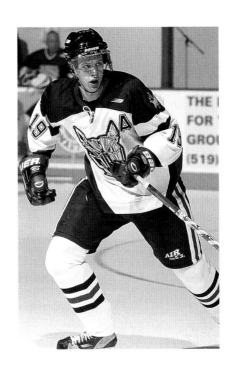

JAYBOUWMEESTER

Scouts will tell you that the most incongruous part of watching Jay Bouwmeester is reconciling his play with the date on his birth certificate — September 27, 1983. Bouwmeester, a defenseman, was already a solid 6-4, 200 by age 15, when he made his Western Hockey League debut with the Medicine Hat Tigers. The next year, he qualified for Canada's world junior team, becoming only the fourth his age to do so after Wayne Gretzky, Eric Lindros and fellow prodigy Jason Spezza. "A Paul Coffey-type, only bigger," says one opposing coach. Rick Carriere, the Tigers coach, adds: "A player like Jay only comes around once in a lifetime." The good news for Carriere and the Tigers is the downside for the NHL. Bouwmeester isn't eligible for the entry draft until 2002. The waiting, as Tom Petty once said, will be the hardest part.

INDEX

PHOTOCREDITS

Cover Photos: Pavel Bure by Doug Pensinger – Allsport, Jaromir Jagr by Rick Stewart – Allsport, Paul Kariya by Robert Leberge – Allsport, Curtis Joseph by Harry How – Allsport.

Back Cover Photos: Robyn Regehr by Jeff Gross – Allsport, Sergei Federov by Rick Stewart – Allsport.

Dustjacket Photos: Pavel Bure by Doug Pensinger – Allsport, Jaromir Jagr by Rick Stewart – Allsport, Paul Kariya by Robert Leberge – Allsport, Curtis Joseph by Harry How – Allsport, Ed Belfour by Aubrey Washington – Allsport, Robyn Regehr by Jeff Gross – Allsport, Sergei Federov by Rick Stewart – Allsport, Steve Yzerman by Robert Laberge – Allsport.

Allsport Photography USA: Steve Babineau: pgs. 10, 25, 92, 95, 124, 125, 144; Brian Bahr: pgs. 20, 23, 26, 34, 35, 36, 37, 59, 61, 90, 108, 116, 117, 119, 145; Al Bello: pgs. 14, 15, 38, 39, 40, 41, 85, 105, 106, 132, 135, 140; Jeff Gross: pgs. 11, 19, 21, 60, 126, 127, 152, 156; Elsa Hasch: pgs. 22, 32, 46, 47, 58, 61, 78, 79, 91, 94, 98, 100, 101, 112, 123, 134, 154, 155; Harry How: pgs. 1, 2, 4, 72, 73, 74, 103, 122, 159; Robert Laberge: pgs. 1, 2, 6, 16, 31, 33, 54, 56, 57, 65, 68, 75, 86, 88, 89, 104, 107, 119, 136, 138, 147, 148, 159; Vincent Laforet: pgs. 5, 42, 43, 121, 123; Kellie Landis: pgs. 3, 9, 11, 17, 19, 27, 28, 29, 52, 53, 66, 77, 79, 87, 99, 102, 103, 127, 129, 141, 142, 146, 151, 156; M. David Leeds: pg. 139; Donald Miralle: pgs. 18, 64, 67; Doug Pensinger: pgs. 5, 8, 80, 81; Tom Pidgeon: pgs. 55, 97, 110, 113; Elliot Schechter: pg. 48; Ezra Shaw: pgs. 101, 118; Rick Stewart: pgs 1, 12, 15, 45, 57, 83, 89, 93, 96, 97, 107, 128, 129, 150, 155, 158; Jamie Squire: pgs. 13, 133; Damain Strohmeyer: pg. 44; Ian Tomlinson: pgs. 1, 24, 27, 50, 51, 62, 63, 69, 70, 71, 82, 83, 95, 109, 111, 113, 114, 115, 120, 131, 135, 143, 149; Todd Warshaw: pg. 49; Aubrey Washington: 76, 84, 87, 158, 160; Nick Wass: pg. 130.

Bruce Bennett Studios: C. Anderson: pg. 157; D. MacMillian: pgs. 30, 33; Brian Winkler: pg. 51.

Double "E" Photography: Eugene Erick: pg. 157.

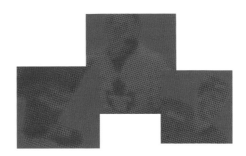

ACKNOWLEDGMENTS

INSPERO PRODUCTIONS INC.

Publishing Director: Marthe Love
Editorial Director: Arthur Pincus
Creative Director: Judy Rudin
Author: Eric Duhatschek
Senior Designer: John Belisle/CDDC
Visual Coordinator: Chris Robertson/CDDC
Design: Belinda Waeland/CDDC
Production Consultant: David Counsell
Executive Assistant: Cynthia Langan/CDDC
Proofreading: Karen Love
Indexing: Cathy Love

We would like to thank all the NHL players for taking the time to answer our questions. Without them, it would have been impossible to present these profiles.

GENERAL ACKNOWLEDGMENTS

Mike Altieri, Los Angeles Kings ● Lindsey Barr ● Bruce Bennett ●
Les Bowen, Chuck Carlton, Tom Jones, Jim Matheson, Allen Panzeri, Al Strachan,
Professional Hockey Writers' Association ● Chris Brown, Carolina Hurricanes ●
Michael Burch, Robert McCullough, Whitecap Books ● Amy Early,
Greg Inglis, Julie O'Sullivan, Adam Schwartz, National Hockey League ●
Robin Evans ● Heidi Holland, Boston Bruins ● Vanessa Lenarduzzi ● Douglas Love ●
Jennifer Love ● Jean Martineau, Colorado Avalanche ● Rick Minch,
New Jersey Devils ● Devin Murray ● Taylor Murray ● Tom Murray ● Rich Nairn,
Phoenix Coyotes ● Peter Orlowsky, Justin Weiss, Allsport Photography ●
Ellen Pincus ● Jay Rosenstein ● Roger Ross, San Jose Sharks ● Jim Taylor ●
Brad Thomas ● Jeff Trammel, St. Louis Blues ● Robert Turner ●